THE CAT WHO CAME TO DINNER

THE CAT WHO CAME TO DINNER

A TRUE RAGS TO RICHES STORY

ELIZABETH DOWNEY

BOOKSMITH PUBLISHING

Published by Booksmith Publishing
www.booksmith.io

Trade Paperback ISBN: 978-1-7359725-0-3
eBook ISBN: 978-1-7359725-1-0

Printed in the United States of America.

To my late Mother,

who adored cats but sacrificed the joy of having one
...because of her daughter's allergies.

Her motto, when approaching anything in life, was:

"Don't procrastinate. Just do it.
Do it now, and do it well!"

So Mother, I've (finally) done it, and here it is!

CONTENTS

PROLOGUE

FELINE. TABBY. MOUSER. CAT. These adorable and mischievous companions go by many names, and I have wanted a cute little fur-ball of my own for as long as I can remember. Growing up with the space constraints of a Manhattan apartment, however, put that dream beyond the realm of possibility. Fortunately, there was a more realistic, albeit temporary, solution to this conundrum: summers at my grand-mother's house in rural Massachusetts.

The house itself sat at the end of a long road, next to a quiet lake in the heart of the Berkshire Mountains. It was the perfect place to escape the hustle and bustle of the city and offered more than enough space for a pet. So, every summer we spent there, I was allowed to find a kitten who could be the family's "furry companion" during our stay.

As soon as we arrived, I would venture over to a nearby farm. The tenant was a local handyman who maintained the summer cottages year-round, and he always had a fresh litter of kittens that I could "borrow" for the coming months. Each summer, I gratefully accepted my new friend and skipped all the way back to the house to introduce it to the rest of the family.

Our temporary kittens over the years always went by either PETRONILLA or PANDORA — two of my mother's favorite names

— to avoid any confusion or mix-ups. Their fur was typically white or beige in color, and they often spent their days under our car, shielding themselves from the sweltering summer heat.

One day, I remember that the car had an oil leak, causing one of the kittens to emerge dazed and confused *(not to mention covered in black grease!)* With the poor thing sulking from its sticky, knotted fur, my mom and I spent the afternoon trying to scrub it off with soapy water. Despite our efforts (and laughter), the previously beige-white kitten ended up looking like a fuzzy, grumpy inkblot.

In addition to lounging around, our kitten friends loved to catch mice and drop them off as small gifts — often leaving them on the back porch as morbid (but generous) surprises. In return, they hoped for praise and doting, not once hesitating to vocalize their annoyance if they did not get any. Of course, at the end of our daily adventures, the kittens and I liked to snuggle up and fall asleep together.

Life was simple back then. I didn't have a care in the world, outside of spending time with my feline friends. But as the summers came to an end, so too did my short-lived dream of having a pet. I dreaded the moment when I would have to bring my kittens back to the farm. Yes, the arrangement was bitter-sweet, but that was the deal. I had my objections, but I knew that I had very little say in the matter. *This was the way it had to be.*

On the way back to the city, and in the days that followed, I almost always experienced some form of congestion. My eyes turned red and itchy, and I found myself sneezing incessantly. My mother wrote off these symptoms as nothing more than pollen allergies. This made sense to me, especially when I thought about how much time I spent outside lying in the grass and picking wildflowers in the Berkshire Mountains. None of us thought that perhaps our summer kittens were the furry culprits behind the onset of these symptoms. However, since everything would clear up within a few days, we never gave it a second thought.

Years later, after my grandmother's death, my mother sold the summer house and the family moved to Connecticut. Strangely, the prospect of getting a permanent cat after the move did not occur to us. Perhaps because we were all so busy adjusting to our new suburban life.

By this time, I had entered my teenage years, which meant *lots* of slumber parties with my friends. In fact, it was not uncommon to have one every weekend. As was customary, all of us brought our own sleeping bags to set up camp in the basement. My friends and I would then chat endlessly into the early hours of the morning and play countless games of TRUTH-OR-DARE. If the friend who was hosting had any pets, they would, of course, join the fun and provide hours of entertainment. Although we never got much sleep, the few hours we *did* manage were spent curled up next to cats and dogs (one of my favorite parts of these get-togethers.)

It was only when I got home from the sleepovers that my troubles would begin. My eyes would water. My nose would seal itself shut from all the congestion. Eventually, I also developed asthma.

My mother became so concerned that she threatened to ban me from attending *all* slumber parties. She was absolutely convinced that these problems were the result of late-night teenage antics and severe sleep deprivation. As one would expect, I begged her to still let me go. In return for her blessing, I promised that I would get more rest. Reluctantly, my mother agreed to this. It was then that I decided to do some detective work to try to identify the *real* culprit behind my symptoms.

In the months that followed, I conducted small experiments, turning down offers for sleepovers if I knew the host had any pets. I was very suspicious that I had developed allergies to animals (or at least those with a lot of fur.) Sure enough, whenever I slept over at an animal-free home, I woke up feeling perfectly fine the next morning.

The one night I made an exception to this rule, I realized that I had made a terrible mistake. After being at a friend's house for just a few hours, I suddenly couldn't breathe. It felt as though someone had their hand around my throat, squeezing all the air from my lungs. Terrified, I called my parents and asked them to come get me. I was certain that this had been a severe allergic reaction to my friend's cat. Wanting to end the debate once and for all, I asked my mother to make an appointment with the doctor to run some tests.

When the results came back and confirmed my suspicions, I was absolutely devastated. I knew, in that moment, that I would never be able to have a cat of my own. Of course, life almost always has a way of surprising us. And 30 years later, I would be the one to have the last laugh.

1

_____

WE MEET

S he walked into my life on a warm, sunny day in January. The year was 1989. With no snow on the ground, it was proving to be an exceptionally mild winter for the Chicago area. For reasons that I cannot recall, I had the day off from work. That morning, I remember peering out the window above the kitchen sink, overlooking the deck and the backyard. That's when I first saw her: *a beautiful, marmalade-colored tabby cat.*

Our backyard was surrounded by woods, and the house made a perfect shield from the wind. Thus, our deck was the ideal spot for this unexpected visitor to lie out in the winter sun and clean herself. I stood there and watched for a while, admiring her thick fur coat and sweet face, which appeared to be frozen in a permanent smile.

She wasn't a skinny cat. In fact, she appeared to be very well-fed. Since cats are known to venture away from home every so often, I figured that she must belong to a neighboring family. Who knows? Perhaps she had decided to go exploring for the day. In any event, after she had been there for a while, I decided to go out and introduce myself. However, I made sure to approach her carefully so as not to scare her off.

To my surprise, the tabby welcomed my presence by purring

loudly and letting me stroke her head and back. During this time, I was able to examine her more closely and noticed that she wasn't wearing a collar. *Well, she may not have any tags around her neck, but she must be from around here,* I thought to myself. Then, I put a bowl of water out, in case she was thirsty. The cat appeared grateful and began to drink from it. Afterward, I forced myself to return to what I was doing inside the house.

I'll admit, it was difficult to get anything done that day, knowing that there was a cat just outside the back door. I was too excited to concentrate on anything other than my newfound friend. Every now and then, I ventured out to the deck to pet and talk with her. Of course, I didn't think she would stick around for the whole day. So, I was surprised to find her still hanging out in the backyard by the time my sons, John (age 10) and James (age 7) got home from school.

As soon as they walked through the front door, I announced, "Boys, I have a surprise for you. You're both going to love this."

"What is it?!" they asked.

"We have a little visitor, and she's out on the deck."

Without a moment's hesitation, both boys squealed in delight and ran to the back of the house. They were eager to see what I was talking about. And it didn't take long before playtime was in full swing.

"She's so friendly! Can we please keep her?" John pleaded.

"She belongs to somebody. See how healthy she is? I'm sure she was just taking a stroll and liked our deck, so she decided to spend the day here," I replied. "Eventually, she'll have to go home, so don't get too attached."

"Mom, we have tuna! Do you think it would be okay to open up a can for her?" James asked.

"Wait a minute. We are *not* going to feed this cat. If she belongs to someone, that wouldn't be right," I warned. "Wouldn't you feel terrible if another family tried to steal your cat by luring it in with food? We can put more water out for her, but *that's it.*"

The boys understood, and we spent the rest of the afternoon

out on the deck, discussing what we should do about our new and unexpected visitor. Despite what I had told James earlier, I found myself wrestling with the idea of feeding her in the hours that followed. When my husband, Bill, came home from work, the boys ran to greet him and deliver the news about our feline friend.

"Dad come look! We have a cat!"

"What do you mean? We don't have a cat," Bill said.

"Well we do now!" the boys exclaimed in unison.

My husband's confusion quickly resolved itself when they pulled him over to the kitchen window and revealed the big orange tabby lounging out there. Despite the fact that Bill was never much of a cat person, he seemed intrigued. Now that they had been introduced, I decided to throw the idea of feeding her out there and get his thoughts on the matter.

"You know, if she sticks around, we *could* give her some food."

"What are you talking about? We can't have a cat. You're allergic to them!" Bill responded, rationally. Then he added, "Besides, everyone knows that once you feed a cat, you have it for life. And cats cost a fortune to take care of."

Just what I had in mind.

Bill had a point: I was terribly allergic to cats. Yet I wasn't concerned about this one. She was clearly comfortable staying outdoors, so I wouldn't have to worry about her fur getting all over the inside of the house. So long as I remembered to wash my hands after our interactions, I could easily manage to keep this tabby around.

It was no secret that I was thrilled to *finally* fulfill my childhood dream of owning a cat. That is, assuming she also wanted to stick around. However, despite my hope that she would remain out on our deck, I was convinced that she would disappear that night. Sure enough, before I went to bed, I peered out the kitchen window.

No sign of her.

7

Since the boys were still awake, I went to deliver the news to them.

"John, James, the cat has gone back to her home."

"I hope she comes back tomorrow," James said.

"I hope so too," I replied and turned out the lights.

2

SHE STAYED

The next morning felt like Christmas. With great excitement and enthusiasm, the boys shook me awake to tell me they were going to see whether the cat had returned. I, too, was eager to discover if our furry friend had come back to us. I grabbed my robe, and we all ran down the stairs — clad in our pajamas — and out the back door.

At first, we saw nothing, and I couldn't help but feel a slight twinge of disappointment. The boys, however, remained optimistic and began to call for her.

"Cat! Oh Ca-aaat! Here kitty, kitty!"

Lo and behold, a few moments later, our cherished companion poked her head out from behind some nearby bushes. Her face expressed nothing but pure joy as if to say, *I'm here!* She then trotted up the steps to greet us.

"Mom, the cat came back!" exclaimed James, crouching down to pet her.

"Does this mean we can stay home from school?" John asked.

"Absolutely not," I said sternly.

"But Mom, if we leave her here all alone, she'll disappear again!"

"You two *cannot* skip school for this," I reiterated. "I'm sure she belongs to another family, but she got a lot of attention from us yesterday. That's probably the reason she came back."

Then I added, "I have to get ready for work, and you boys have to get dressed in time to catch the bus. If the cat wants to stay, she'll be here when you get home from school." With that, I ushered the boys back inside to get ready for the day.

———

BEFORE I LEFT for work that morning, I made sure to put out more water and say goodbye to our new friend. She responded with a little meow as a *thank you* and returned to sunning herself on one of the nearby deck chairs. Meanwhile, I resisted the urge to call in sick for the day and forced myself out the front door.

3

THEN THERE WERE TWO

That afternoon, the boys and I arrived home around the same time. Without saying a word, we all ran to the back-yard to see if our cat friend had stayed. Imagine our surprise when we discovered that not only was she still there, she also was not alone. Another, almost identical cat had joined her!

Our original furry friend came up and greeted us warmly. The second cat, however, did not seem as pleased by our presence. He promptly made his way to the far side of the deck to create some distance between us and himself, looking annoyed as he did so. His friend had obviously neglected to tell him that she had adopted the owners of their new favorite lounge spot — *and he was not happy about it.*

I warned the boys not to get too close to this second cat, as I wasn't sure whether he would bite or scratch if approached. They agreed. We respected our new companion's personal space by remaining on the opposite side of the deck. During that time, we debated over whether the two cats were related.

It was uncanny how similar they looked, causing us to wonder about the nature of their relationship. Ultimately, we concluded that this new cat must be the son of the female tabby, as he was a bit smaller than her and behaved a lot like a stand-offish teenager. Not only did he have a tough demeanor, but he also had rather large paws. Based on this observation, I assumed that this cat was still on the younger side and would one day outgrow his mother.

At this point, the boys and I began to wonder where CAT #2 had come from.

Clearly, word got out that this is a great place to stay, I thought. *How long will it be before all the cats in the neighborhood start spending their days on our back deck?*

In any case, with two cats hanging around the house, it was clear that we needed to come up with names to tell them apart.

"You know, boys, now that we have two furry visitors, we can't keep calling them CAT #1 and CAT #2."

The boys agreed, so I continued, "She seems a lot like a mom, especially now that this young teenage cat is around. So, what if we just call her MOMCAT?"

"Oh, that's good! I like that!" James said.

Even though the name MOMCAT was the first idea that came to mind, the boys thought that it was a perfect fit. Besides, we were certain that she was the mother of the other cat. Now, it was time to find a name for CAT #2.

"Well, the new cat is like a smaller version of Momcat, and he's her son. So, what if we call him JUNIOR?" John suggested.

We all nodded our heads in agreement: *Junior it was.*

"Is everyone happy with the new names for our friends?" I asked.

"Yes!" said the boys.

That was that. From then on, our pair of tabby cats would affectionately be known as Momcat and Junior. As expected, Momcat seemed pleased with her nickname and responded when called. Junior, on the other hand, was indifferent. Now that they both had names, it was time to get to know our new friends a little better.

IT DIDN'T TAKE LONG for us to get a sense for Junior's mannerisms and personality, which differed vastly from that of Momcat's. She had been both friendly and approachable since the beginning, while Junior preferred to keep to himself and observe from a distance. His guard went up the moment any of us attempted to approach him. And while he never hissed or scratched, he made it clear, early on, that he would not tolerate any petting.

I found it amusing how these two cats appeared almost identical yet had such opposing personalities. Not only did Momcat enjoy snuggling up to us, but she also liked to convey her contentment with lots of meows and incessant purring. Whenever we would speak to her, she responded as though she understood exactly what was being said. This made it easy to bond with her, whereas with Junior, that was not the case. We never heard him utter a purr nor any other sound for that matter.

Every move he made seemed carefully calculated, and he always kept a wary eye on everyone as if skeptical of our intentions. There was very little interaction between him and the rest of us. Given his cold temperament, however, that was perfectly fine.

The boys continued to play with Momcat, while I went to fetch a fresh bowl of water for our two feline friends. Then I watched as our beloved Momcat drank from it with her usual appreciation. Junior, of course, waited until the boys and I backed away — leaving him plenty of room — before he made his way over to the bowl. As his head bent over the water, I noticed that he, too, had no collar or ID tags.

How strange, I thought. It was at that moment that I made an important, life-changing decision for our family: *I would begin feeding the cats.*

It wouldn't be much — just enough to supplement their current diet, as I still wasn't sure whether they belonged to another family. For all we knew, these cats could have been "working the system" and trying to double their daily food allowance. Even if that were the case, it didn't bother me. I wanted them to stick around. And naturally, my mothering instincts got the better of me. I began plotting to pick up some kibble before Bill came home.

"I think I'm going to swing by the pet store to buy some food," I said.

"Oh! Can we come too?" James asked.

"Of course, you can. This is a secret mission though, okay boys?"

"Daddy's not going to be very happy about this," said John.

"It's just a little cat food. How much can it really cost?" I replied, laughing.

With that, the boys shrieked in excitement and ran to the car. I went inside to grab my purse and keys. Minutes later, we were on our way.

I had often passed the local pet store on my way to work, so I knew where I had to go. Upon arriving, the boys and I went inside and sought out the owner. I explained to him that two cats had adopted us, and we wanted to have something for them to eat. He recommended a brand that was high in nutrition in case they were not getting food elsewhere.

"What if they don't like it?" I asked.

"Then I would recommend buying two or three different varieties for them to try. It may require some trial and error, but you will know very quickly what they like and dislike."

"Should I be concerned that they live outdoors? I mean, they seem fine with it, but I worry about their exposure to the cold."

"These cats are capable of surviving outdoors, especially during a warm winter like this. Besides, their thick fur will keep them warm," he assured me.

By the end of the exchange, I walked out of there with two bags of cat food as well as some proper bowls to serve it from. According to the store owner, this would be enough to last two weeks. *Hopefully, now they will stick around a while...so long as the food is agreeable,* I thought, crossing my fingers.

Five minutes later, we were back home from our secret mission. We walked through the front door and noticed that Bill had returned from work. Right away, the cat was out of the bag.

"Guess what, Dad? We just bought some food for the kitties!" James announced.

"*Oh great,*" my husband responded, rolling his eyes. "Now these cats will never leave."

"But Dad, we couldn't let them starve! They're ours now!" James said, defensively.

"Yes. I'm sure they will be our cats *now,*" Bill muttered under his breath.

The boys clapped their hands with glee and ran to the kitchen to start preparing the food for Momcat and Junior. Afterward, we went outside, set the bowls down, and waited. In a matter of seconds, Junior had rushed over from his corner of the deck and stuck his nose straight into the kibble. Momcat followed close behind. Then, once the food had disappeared, so did our cats...out into the night.

4

THE ADVENTURES OF MOMCAT AND JUNIOR

I n the days that followed, we began to adjust to our new, day-to-day lives with the tabbies. Both Momcat and Junior turned out to be early risers. This meant that they were almost always up on the deck to greet us by the time we were ready to start the day. When the boys and I went outside to feed them, Momcat would wish us a pleasant *good morning* by meowing and purring. As for Junior, he continued to keep his distance (unless there was food to be had), shooting sideways glances in our direction every now and then.

Outside mealtimes, the cats would lounge around on the deck. They enjoyed sunning themselves on the patio furniture and sleeping excessively. They also liked grooming their immaculate marmalade fur and scanning for birds, squirrels, and other small animals. *Typical cat activities.* They even took pleasure in piling inside a nearby empty planter, which offered extra protection from the winter wind. But, of course, mealtimes were the most anticipated part of each day.

The owner of the pet store had recommended I feed the cats twice daily: once in the morning and again in the afternoon. However, I was inclined to offer more of a "full-service restaurant" to our two little companions. This meant that, if I was home, their food and water bowls would be replenished throughout the day. If I had to go to work, then the cats had to make do with their morning chow and wait until I got home for the white-glove service to resume.

For me, the most amusing part of this routine was seeing how quickly Junior's demeanor would change. Without fail, he would abandon his typical sourpuss self the moment he heard me pick up the food bowl to refill it. I have never seen a cat so enthusiastic in my life! He would always rush over from his corner of the deck, as if to say, *Hey, I'm here! Ready for my breakfast!* Then, he would wait impatiently for me to set down the bowl overflowing with delicious kibble. At which point, he would go into a frenzy — like a cat possessed — and do an immediate nosedive into the bowl. Nothing in the world could bother Junior while he was devouring his food, not even a few pats on the back from me and the boys. Momcat, on the other hand, was never as ravenous as Junior and often took her time moseying over to the food after it was served.

At this point, our family's life was consumed by watching and interacting with our new friends during the day and speculating as to where the tabbies went at night. Every evening, like clockwork, both Momcat and Junior would disappear shortly after dinner. Yet, none of us had any idea where they were going. I suspected that they weren't traveling too far, since they always showed up on our deck early the next morning. While the possibility remained that they had another home, I often worried about their safety once the sun went down. After all, our suburb was no stranger to deer, raccoons, and other wild creatures.

To bribe them into sticking around after dark, I decided to put out an extra bowl of food before going to bed each night. One evening, James noticed me doing this and proudly exclaimed, "Now our cats will have food around the clock. Just like a 24-hour diner!"

"I know, I'm a softy," I said, laughing. "I just don't want them to go hungry."

Famous last words.

It didn't take long before other animals took notice of the

food I left out for the cats. A few nights later, while Bill and I were watching TV, we heard a terrible commotion out on the deck. There were many hisses and angry, animal-like screeches coming from what sounded like Junior. We ran to the kitchen and flipped on the outdoor lights. That's when we saw it: *the intruder*, a sizable opossum, attempting to ransack the bowl of kibble. He must have wanted a meal at our all-night diner.

A few inches away stood Junior, baring his teeth and uttering all kinds of terrible noises. Momcat also stood ready for battle but stayed behind her son. I turned to Bill and asked, "Who do you think is going to win?"

He shook his head in response, and I prepared to go out and defend my cats.

Apparently, no intervention was needed. Junior, who was not at all intimidated, began to advance towards the creature, swiping at it with his enormous paws. The trespasser responded by slowly backing away from the bowl before turning and running toward the woods.

Victory! Junior had successfully safeguarded his midnight snack. And he seemed pleased with himself over his banishment of the uninvited guest.

I went out to check on both cats before calling it a night. Momcat needed comforting after all the chaos, so I gave her some pets while praising Junior for his excellent work. After that, I went back inside and headed upstairs — all the while wondering how the cats had detected the opossum up on the deck. *Surely, they must have been somewhere nearby.*

But regardless of how they had become aware of the situation, I knew one thing for sure: I didn't want our beloved tabbies having any more run-ins with rogue suburban animals. So, I made an executive decision to limit the hours of our all-night diner after that.

The next morning, we finally solved the mystery of the cats' sleeping arrangements. I went out to feed them but noticed that they weren't on the deck. My heart sank as I thought about what had happened the night before. *Were they attacked after I went to bed?*

However, just before my thoughts took a turn for the worse, I saw a little marmalade head pop out from behind some nearby bushes. Curious, I walked over to get a closer look. That's when I noticed that both cats were emerging from beneath our deck.

The deck itself was raised about a foot off the ground, which left just enough clearance for Momcat and Junior to get in and out from under it.

There wasn't much down there, aside from some soft earth and a basement window. Yet it provided plenty of shelter from the elements. It was also close to our full-service restaurant, making it the perfect set of accommodations for two outdoor cats.

They must have been sleeping under there the whole time, I thought. *What smart tabbies!*

THE SEARCH

Momcat and Junior showed no signs of leaving. In fact, they seemed to enjoy the routine we had all established. And we were thrilled that the tabbies wanted to stick around. Even Bill was starting to warm up to them, often giving them a pat or two before leaving for work in the morning. However, despite feeling like the cats were now *ours,* I still wanted to find out where they had come from. More importantly, I wanted to make sure that there wasn't another family out looking for them.

To start, I decided to call the local veterinarian to determine if he had any possible leads. The initial call, however, didn't yield much useful information. First, I explained that two beautiful tabbies had showed up one day and were sleeping under our deck. Then I asked if he knew of anyone who might have lost their cats.

"No one that I know of," the vet responded. "But I will keep it in mind in case anyone shows up asking about them."

The next step was to try the pet store. I stopped by on my way home from work and asked the owner if he knew of anyone whose cats had gone missing. He hadn't heard anything, so I asked him to keep an eye out and headed back to the house.

At this point, the only thing left to do was to create flyers and post them around the neighborhood. The flyers read:

TWO STRIPED CATS FOUND, BOTH TABBIES

ONE MALE, ONE FEMALE. MARMALADE IN COLOR.

THE FEMALE IS FULL-GROWN. THE MALE IS ALMOST
GROWN BUT SMALLER.

IF YOU HAVE ANY INFORMATION, PLEASE CONTACT LIZ
DOWNEY.

John, James, and I then set to work distributing the flyers anywhere we could. We tacked them up on utility poles, stuffed them in mailboxes, and pinned them to bulletin boards at stores around town. With help from the boys, the whole process took about a day to complete. Afterward, all we could do was to sit and wait for that dreaded phone call from Momcat and Junior's real family.

In the days that followed, every time the phone rang, our hearts would stop. The boys were certain that it was someone calling to claim our beloved new pets. At one point, I remember James saying, "If they *do* belong to someone else, couldn't we just give *one* of them back and keep the other?"

Of course, none of us wanted to see the cats go, but we knew that this was the right thing to do. Luckily, all the phone calls we received were from neighbors who had seen the flyers and wondered if we wanted to give the cats away. I told them we weren't interested.

Despite our outreach attempts, no one ever claimed Momcat or Junior. So, as the days went on, we became more confident that they would continue living with us.

A week later, the calls died out. Now, we had exhausted all efforts to learn whether our feline friends had indeed had a previous residence. At least for the time being, the cats were here to stay.

A ROAD TRIP FOR MOMCAT AND JUNIOR

To ensure that the new additions to our family were healthy, I scheduled a trip to the vet. This way, the cats could have their checkups and get the necessary vaccinations. Of course, the veterinarian already knew the backstory of Momcat and Junior and was eager to meet them in person. He was so eager, in fact, that he asked to see them the very next day.

Making the appointments was the easy part. Now, I had to figure out how to transport the tabbies to, and from, the vet's office. However, the task proved to be a challenging one. I had to consider the fact that these cats had never been anywhere other than the outdoors. Because of this, I was concerned about how they would react once confined to the inside of my car.

Even though the trip would be a short one, it was difficult to predict what the cats would do when removed from their natural environment. For all I knew, ten minutes of restricted freedom could have been an eternity from a stray cat's perspective.

I figured that Momcat would most likely be fine, given her easy-going nature. Junior, however, would probably go berserk. I also couldn't have the two of them climbing all over the car and distracting me from the road. The trunk wasn't an option either (for obvious reasons.) After much deliberation, I came up with a simple solution: a delivery box.

If I could get both cats into a decent-sized box — outfitted with some windows and air holes — then I at least had *a chance* of making the trip successful. In all honesty, I didn't know what else to do. Yes, I could have gone out and bought a cat carrier, but it didn't make sense to invest in one for two outdoor tabbies, who rarely left the backyard.

With my mind made up, I headed to the basement to search for a box to use. I found one that was the perfect size for the occasion: a sturdy, two-by-two-foot cardboard crate that had arrived in the mail a week before. Not only did it have the right dimensions, but it was also easy to open and easy to close. Hauling it upstairs, I called for John and James to help me get it ready for the tabbies.

"I'm taking Momcat and Junior to the vet tomorrow, and I want to use this cardboard box to get them there."

"But Mom, they won't be able to breathe inside that thing!" said James, with a great deal of concern.

"That's why I need you boys to help me. We are going to poke some holes and cut out a few windows so that the cats don't suffocate."

"Nothing bad is going to happen to the kitties, James," John reassured.

"Okay. As long as my cats can breathe, I'll help," James replied.

With both boys on board, I brought the cardboard box into the kitchen and set to work. It turned out that my sons were excellent architects. They carefully poked out quarter-sized holes and carved out windows that were big enough to ease any feline claustrophobia — but not *so big* that the cats would be able to jump out.

Within 30 minutes, we had created a functional means of transport. Now, it was only a matter of convincing the cats to get *in*.

That night, I cooked up a plan to lure Momcat and Junior into the box, while mentally preparing myself for the upcoming occasion.

THE NEXT MORNING, I woke up early and opened a can of tuna. Then I placed it at the bottom of our makeshift cat carrier and scooped some out to bait Junior. By this time, the boys were also awake and assisted me in bringing the box out to the deck.

As expected, Momcat was the easy one. She allowed James to lift her up and place her inside the box without protest.

Now it was Junior's turn. I walked over to his side of the deck and bent down to let him lick some tuna off my fingers. The bribe worked perfectly. Junior wanted more and followed as I walked back across the deck, holding my tuna fingers as close to his nose as possible.

Carefully, I dropped the remaining pieces into the box and watched him stand on his hind legs to peer over the edge. He must have *really* wanted that tuna because he didn't object when I picked him up and plopped him down next to Momcat.

Worried that my luck might soon run out, I told the boys to quickly close up the top so that I could secure the enclosure with some duct tape. *Oh, the betrayal they must have felt once the top was on.*

Everything was going according to plan...that is, until the cats ran out of tuna.

At this point, chaos ensued as Junior began to panic. The box shook furiously. It became so unsteady, in fact, that it took all three of us to lug the thing over to the car and load it into the backseat. Now, it seemed the hardest part was over. The boys stayed behind, and I hopped into the driver's seat.

That's when the shrieking started.

Before the keys were even in the ignition, Junior decided that if he could not escape this cardboard prison, he would make sure that everyone within a five-block radius knew how ticked off he was.

The next ten minutes were pure pandemonium. I did my best to focus on the road, but whenever I checked the rearview mirror, all I could see were cat limbs. I also caught a glimpse of

Junior's angry face poking out of every possible opening. He howled and shrieked in protest the entire way, not once taking a break to refill his lungs with air.

Worried that he might soon break through the duct tape, I began using the most soothing voice I could muster. All I wanted was to help Junior calm down. Meanwhile, Momcat seemed perfectly content with everything that had transpired up to this point. *Thank goodness I only have to comfort one agitated cat and not two,* I thought.

Just as I was about to go nuts from Junior's cries ringing in my ears, we pulled up to the veterinarian's office. Having been made aware of the situation ahead of time, the receptionist was waiting in the parking lot to help usher both cats inside.

We made it through the front door, and she led me straight to the exam room. From there, the next step was to unload the tabbies. It seemed easy enough, at first, but ended up resulting in quite a scene.

Before I could finish pulling the duct tape off the top, the flaps flew open and out shot Junior like a rogue missile. He landed with a heavy *THUD!* on the linoleum floor and made a break for the door. *(No doubt, he was ready to zoom down the hallway and get as far away from this strange place as possible.)* However, Junior's attempts to liberate himself were thwarted by the vet, who just happened to be coming in to see us at that precise moment.

"Hey, little fella! Where are you going?" he asked, scooping Junior up with his free hand.

Taking a few steps into the room, he then closed the door behind him and set Junior down again. "We'll just let him roam around for a bit until he calms down."

"That's an excellent idea," I said, then lifted Momcat out of the box and set her down on the exam table. I was delighted by how well she was behaving and, of course, was grateful for her cooperation.

"Who do we have here?" the vet asked.

"Well, we've been calling her Momcat, but we don't know for sure if she's a female. The unruly one over there is Junior."

The veterinarian looked her over and confirmed that I had correctly guessed the sex. He then checked Momcat for any signs of fleas or worms before giving her the necessary shots. She handled the entire thing like a champ.

Meanwhile, Junior remained in a constant state of motion. Jumping up and down from any and every surface in the room, it was clear that he was desperately seeking a means of escape. But before he could find any viable exit points, his efforts were once again thwarted by the vet, who picked him up and placed him on the table. I struggled to hold Junior still as the doctor performed his checks.

"Both cats are in perfect health," he announced.

"That's wonderful news," I said. "You know, I'm actually allergic to cats, so these two spend all of their time outside. Is that okay? I mean, do you think there is any risk of them freezing to death?"

"Don't worry about that," he replied. "These cats have some of the thickest fur I've ever seen. They'll be fine staying outdoors."

I thanked the vet for his time, and he helped me get the cats back into the bulky, homemade carrier. Together, we then hauled it out to the car. Fortunately, the return trip was not nearly as bad. Junior had calmed down quite a bit but continued to protest his cardboard jail cell.

When we pulled into the garage, I immediately opened the box and took him out first. He allowed me to return him to the deck, then waited for me to fetch Momcat.

Once both tabbies were back outside, I rewarded them with some food. I crossed my fingers that neither would end up with psychological trauma after what they had just endured. However, a few minutes of watching them eat and roam about put my mind at ease. At least for the moment, all was right with the world.

7

UPSCALE HOUSING FOR THE
TABBIES

U p until February, the winter weather had been mild and
warm enough to ease my conscience about leaving the
cats outdoors. Whenever it rained, both tabbies took refuge
below the deck. When the sun came out, Momcat would fall
asleep on her favorite bench. Meanwhile, Junior used the opportunity to explore the woods — often disappearing for hours at a
time.

The boys and I were never quite sure *what* he did during his
adventures, but we had a hunch that he was supplementing his
current diet with a variety of field mice.

From time to time, I wondered whether Junior would return
from these mini hunting excursions. He always seemed to be
roaming around, looking for trouble. Whether he came back for
the comforts of his new home or for Momcat, I could never be
sure. But he always returned, and for that, I was grateful.

One particular morning, while I was away at work, it began
to snow. This was the first real blizzard of the year. The snow
itself was heavy and wet, almost like sludge.

From the moment it started, my nurturing instincts took
over. All I could think about was that the cats' thick fur coats
would soon become water-logged, which might make them cold

27

and sick. The thought continued to gnaw at me as the day went on.

By the time lunch rolled around, I had to do *something*. I told my assistant to cancel my afternoon meetings and headed out to the car.

The drive home was a long one. My mind raced with all kinds of questions and scenarios.

Do the cats know to go below the deck to stay dry? Will they end up sick? Would I have to make another trip to the vet?

I couldn't stand the thought of keeping them outside in this kind of weather. I also knew that I couldn't bring them inside the house and risk having a severe allergic reaction. So, I made up my mind to get Momcat and Junior a more robust residence. That way, they would be better protected against the Chicago winter going forward.

Minutes later, I pulled up to the pet store and ran inside to find the owner.

"Hello again, I remember you!" the owner said as soon as he saw me.

"Hi!" I responded, trying to catch my breath. "Do you have any cat houses? Like a doghouse but for cats?"

He laughed. "I've never heard of houses made for cats, but I *do* have some doghouses that might work."

"I'll take whatever you think will accommodate two adult tabbies."

"I know just the one," the owner replied.

The doghouse he selected was approximately the same size as our makeshift cat carrier but stood a little taller. Its walls were cream-colored, and there was a green, slanted roof that could be detached if needed. Additionally, the whole thing was made of heavy plastic, which meant that it would be sturdy enough to withstand the wind. An opening had been cut out of the front to allow the cats a point of entry. It was exactly what I had in mind.

Satisfied, I thanked the owner for his help and made the purchase. The two of us then loaded it into the back of the car, and I continued on my way.

By the time I reached the house, only a few inches of snow had fallen — but it was still coming down hard. I managed to haul the cats' new shelter out to the deck, where I positioned it against the house. Shortly after that, John and James arrived home from school and saw this latest addition to the backyard.

"Do they have anything soft to lay on in there?" James asked.

"Yeah, the kitties need a blanket or pillow to sleep on," said John.

"What about James' old quilt? That would be perfect for them," I suggested.

"Okay!" the boys agreed, and I went to fetch it from the closet.

Together, the three of us went outside and pulled the roof off the doghouse. I then placed the blanket at the bottom, making sure that every corner of the floor was covered.

Momcat and Junior watched as we put the roof back on and began encouraging them to test out their new accommodations. Both, however, seemed quite content sitting out in the snow.

To help them better understand what was happening, I went over to pick up Momcat. I then proceeded to set her down in front of the entrance to the little residence.

"This is your new home now," I said. "See how nice and toasty it is inside? Now you won't have to worry about getting your fur wet from the snow."

Intrigued, Momcat began to wander around the interior, then curled up on the comforter. But before the boys and I could celebrate this success, she came back out on the deck.

"Why didn't she stay inside? Doesn't she like it?" James asked.

"Well, it's still very new to them, honey. They need more time to get used to it."

We made several attempts to help the cats get better acquainted with their upgraded residence, but it was no use. Neither Momcat nor Junior seemed interested in spending any time "indoors." However, they were still curious, and took several walks around the perimeter of the doghouse — sniffing the walls as they did so.

Not long after, Bill came home, and we all went inside to warm up. After dinner and a round of hot cocoa, I put the boys to bed and went back outside to check on the tabbies. To further bribe them into spending the night in the doghouse, I brought them a pillow to sleep on.

Once again, I placed Momcat inside the residence and covered her with James' old quilt, which she, of course, shook off. A minute later, she got up and walked out, returning to her place on the snow-covered deck. Meanwhile, Junior remained in his little corner and watched the whole process play out. Neither of them could be bothered to adjust their lifestyle — winter weather be damned! Frustrated, I threw my hands up and called it a night.

The morning after the snowstorm, I returned to the deck only to discover both cats draped, side-by-side, over the roof of the doghouse. My first thought? *I can't believe that I bought this thing, and now these two are using it as a perch!* But seeing how happy they were up there, my irritation quickly subsided. The whole scene was actually quite amusing, especially when I noticed a smile on Momcat's sweet face.

At least both cats seem comfortable enough to sit on top of the doghouse, I told myself. *That's a good starting point. Besides, we can work on getting them to appreciate the inside later on.*

8

FROM TWO CATS TO SEVEN

By the time March rolled around, the whole family had
grown tired of the Chicago cold. Fortunately, we had made
plans to spend spring break skiing in Colorado. Not wanting to
abandon the cats for two weeks (and fearing that they might not
stick around), I asked a neighbor to look after them while we
were away.

Everything seemed normal upon our return, but also inex-
plicably different. In all the weeks that Junior had been with us,
he had always kept his distance from the family. Yet, after our
short time away, one almost got the impression that he had
missed us. He began to let down his guard and allow the boys
and I to approach him.

Junior wasn't the only one who had changed, however. Something also seemed different about Momcat. She greeted us with
the usual pleasantries but looked as though she had put on some
weight while we were away. I naïvely dismissed this as the
neighbor overfeeding her. Little did I know that she had had a
little spring break celebration of her own...and gotten *frisky* with
one of the neighborhood cats.

BY LATE APRIL, it was clear that Momcat was well on her way to having kittens. This, of course, introduced a whole new set of challenges for us to contend with.

What would we do with all of these babies? Who was the father? When would the births occur? Would we have to help with the delivery?

I had so many questions and concerns that I decided it was time to consult with a professional. So, with Momcat's belly nearly touching the ground, I called to make an appointment with the veterinarian for that afternoon.

The trip over was easy enough. I loaded Momcat into the cardboard cat carrier and placed her in the backseat. As usual, she remained cool and collected, entirely unfazed by our travels.

We arrived at the vet's office ten minutes later and walked in.

"What brings you in this time around?" the veterinarian asked.

"Well I can't tell if this cat is just getting fat from all the food that I've been feeding her, or if she's pregnant," I replied, laughing.

"Alright, go ahead and set her on the table, and we'll check to make sure that everything is okay."

I did as he instructed and, after a few minutes of inspecting her stomach, he confirmed my suspicions.

"She is, in fact, pregnant and in great health. She'll be ready to deliver in about a month."

Hearing this news was both exciting and anxiety-inducing. I had no idea how to care for her during the pregnancy, let alone after the kittens arrive. Immediately, I began firing off questions and consulting with the vet on next steps.

Would she be alright staying outside throughout all of this? Will she be able to deliver the babies herself or will I need to intervene? If she has them under the deck, would I be able to assist her?

"She'll be fine," he assured me. "Cats have been doing this for a long time, so she will know what to do. You won't have to intervene in any way. Also, she probably won't have the babies under the deck."

"If she doesn't have them there, then where will she go?"

"Someplace close, but it will not be where she and Junior have been sleeping. Going elsewhere will give her more privacy during the delivery."

"You don't think Junior is the father, do you?"

"Not likely. When they were in here last time, I got the sense that he came from her first litter. That said, he hasn't matured enough to start fathering children. Chances are, this pregnancy resulted from a rendezvous with another cat in the neighborhood."

"Well, that answers *that*. I was wondering how all this happened," I said with a chuckle. "How many kittens do you think she'll have?"

"It's difficult to say...five or six?"

Six cats! What are we going to do with six cats?!

The veterinarian must have noticed the bewildered expression on my face because he repeated that everything would be fine.

"Just take this one day at a time," he said, as he helped load Momcat back into her box and bring her out to the car.

I wasn't so sure but thanked him anyway for his counsel and headed home.

Both Bill and the boys were at the house by the time I got back, so I broke the news to the whole family at once:

"We're having kittens!"

"Kittens!" John and James shouted in unison, clapping their hands.

"These cats are starting to rack up quite a debt," my husband joked...before addressing the *real* elephant in the room.

"Cost aside, what are you going to do when the kittens arrive? If they continue living outdoors, and it starts to rain, you won't be able to bring them inside. If you do, your allergies will flare up. How are you going to deal with that?"

"I don't know, but the cats have been doing well up to this point. They sleep under the deck, and they have their doghouse," I replied, thinking out loud.

"You're asking the right questions, Bill, but I don't want to think about the answers right now. I just want to enjoy this wonderful news."

With that, the topic was dropped, and the conversation went back to the upcoming births and how we would best prepare for them.

———

THE KITTENS WERE BORN on a Saturday morning in late May. The sun had barely risen when I awoke to some commotion coming from the backyard. Curious, I walked over to the bedroom window to see what was going on. That's when I saw Momcat. She was carrying a tiny orange kitten in her mouth and heading towards the house. Seconds later, she scooted under the deck with her baby.

Not wanting to disturb her process, I remained at the window and watched. Once again, Momcat emerged and trotted back across the yard over to a tree at the edge of the woods. The tree's trunk bore a good-sized knot hole about three feet from the ground. It was this hole that served as a safe haven for Momcat to deliver her litter of kittens.

Mesmerized, I observed as she made her way up the tree and fetched another baby — this one had beige fur! Picking it up by the back of its neck, Momcat jumped down from the hole and began the journey back.

At this point, I was unable to contain my excitement. I ran to wake the boys and Bill so that the whole family could witness this fascinating process unfold. We stood watch from the upstairs windows so as not to frighten Momcat in any way. There was lots of *ooh*-ing and *aah*-ing as we saw her travel back and forth across the yard. Each time, she ferried a tiny kitten to safety beneath the deck.

Junior was nowhere in sight, but we assumed that he was looking after the litter while Momcat dealt with the transfers. In total, she made five trips, which meant five babies! Three of which were orange, like their mother, and two with creamy beige fur. Once the last kitten was safe under the deck, Momcat disappeared for the rest of the day.

For hours after the births, the only thing the boys and I could talk about was how resourceful Momcat had been. Who would've thought that a cat would select a tree hole to deliver her babies? What a wonderful, safe place for her kittens!

Sometime later that afternoon, Junior came up on the deck, looking for his dinner. He ate hastily before disappearing again.

It wasn't until the next morning that Momcat resurfaced to drink some water and have her breakfast. She then returned to her babies. Junior, on the other hand, skipped breakfast but showed up for lunch. That's when we realized that they were taking turns and alternating meals so that one cat could safeguard the little ones at all times. Once again, I found myself thinking, *What smart tabbies!*

I had read somewhere that nursing mothers keep their kittens close and are very protective for the first six weeks. Because of this, I knew it would be a while before any of us got a chance to see the new babies. All we could do for now was wait for the cat family to emerge. However, one of the kittens had a more *expedited* timeline in mind.

9

JAMES TO THE RESCUE

Five weeks had passed since the kittens joined our family. Momcat and Junior continued to take turns looking after the little ones, so that the "liberated" party could come up for food and water. Beyond that, we had very little interaction with any member of the cat family, making our backyard feel eerily quiet. Not even the kittens made a sound, which I found a bit odd. Nevertheless, we gave both parents and children plenty of space to carry on with their day-to-day routines. All the while we eagerly anticipated the first opportunity to meet the five new kitties.

The moment came sooner than expected when, early one morning, I awoke to the distressed meows of Momcat. These meows were accompanied by a symphony of tiny squeaks that seemed to come from one of the kittens. Worried that someone was either hurt or in trouble, I rushed over to the bedroom window to look down at the deck. The sun had yet to rise, so it was difficult to see much of anything. All I could make out was Momcat's silhouette, pacing back and forth near the window well.

As her cries became more frantic, I decided to wake Bill and enlist his help in investigating the situation further. Together, we went downstairs and headed outside. Within seconds of our arrival, we heard baby squeaks coming from below the deck.

"Oh no, something must be wrong with one of the kittens!" I fretted.

"I think so too, but how are we going to get under the deck to see what the problem is?" Bill asked.

That's when we both noticed that Momcat was looking over the edge of the window well and trying to communicate with something down there. At that point, Bill and I were quite confused and had a hard time seeing anything in the dark. So, we went inside to grab a flashlight before walking across the deck to check on the situation.

For context, the opening of the window well was located at the top of the deck and went down approximately four feet to the basement. Its sole purpose was to let natural light into the cellar during the day. Covering the top of the well was a clear, plastic dome, which Bill had put in place years before so that the boys wouldn't accidentally fall in. Somehow, one of the orange kittens had managed to fall into this hollowed out area and was now trapped. It was now up to us to carry out a pre-sunrise rescue mission.

In addition to its depth, the window well was rather narrow. This meant that it was almost impossible to get a ladder down there, let alone a person. Nevertheless, both of us tried getting on our stomachs and reaching over the edge to get a hold of the kitten. Unfortunately, neither Bill nor I had arms that were long enough.

Our next idea was to try one of Bill's fishing nets. We both had a hunch that the handle would be long enough to reach the bottom of the well, which would allow us to scoop the kitten up from there. The net also had a fishy smell, which we figured might help convince the kitten to crawl in. I ran to the garage to fetch it and, ten minutes later, we were faced with yet another failed attempt. Now, we had no choice but to wake John and James to enlist their help.

Since the boys were still young, we assumed that one of them might be able to fit into the hard-to-reach areas of the well, either from the opening at the top or from the basement window. After some deliberation, the decision was to start with the basement, as it seemed like the easier option.

The whole family marched down the stairs and over to the window where the kitty was stuck. Sure enough, there it was: a tiny orange tabby, all curled up in a corner opposite the window. There was no way for it to climb out, so the only thing the kitten could do was to cry out repeatedly. The poor thing seemed so scared and helpless. It was heartbreaking to watch.

Each one of us tried to pry the window open, but it wouldn't budge. The previous owners of the house had painted over the trim, making it near impossible to move either the handle or the hinges.

At this point, I said, "If we can't get this, we may have to break the window."

To which my husband replied, "There is *no way* that is going to happen."

"But we have to get this cat out!"

"We are not going to take apart this house for these cats."

"Then what if we called the fire department? They rescue pets all the time," I suggested.

"I'm not a fan of that idea either," Bill said.

"I just don't see any other way," I replied.

That's when James chimed in. "Wait, I think I can fit down there!"

"Oh sweetie, I don't know if that's such a good idea."

"We have to try!"

Without waiting for a response, James ran upstairs. Despite our initial hesitation, Bill and I figured it was worth a shot. (Not to mention, we were running out of ideas.)

Back up on the deck, we removed the dome covering. Then, John and I took one of James' arms while Bill took the other. Together, the three of us slowly lowered him down into the window well.

Throughout the chaos, Junior and the other kittens were nowhere to be seen. Meanwhile, Momcat continued to pace back and forth on the deck, meowing incessantly to communicate how upset she was. She watched our various attempts to recover her baby and seemed to understand that we wanted to help. But when James began his descent into the well, she became more interested in supervising the situation. She quickly made her way between John's legs, peering over the edge of the tin fitting to get a better view.

Once James reached the bottom, it was clear that even with his thin body, this would be a tight fit. There wasn't much room to maneuver, but that didn't stop him from trying to squat down and pick up the frightened little tabby.

"I can't reach him," we heard him say. "He keeps moving away from me!"

"Let's give James the fishing net and try that," John suggested.

"Excellent idea!" I said, and slid the net down the side of the well.

James grabbed it. After a bit of fumbling to get the net into position, he managed to scoop the kitten up and hand it back to me. From there, I slowly lowered both net and kitten — who had his little paws tangled up in the mesh — down onto the deck's surface. Meanwhile, Bill and John lifted James out of the well. I'm sure our cheers could be heard down the street as we celebrated our success.

"Be careful not to touch the kitty," I reminded everyone.

"Why not?" asked John.

"Because I read somewhere that nursing mothers will not take their kittens back if they've been touched by humans. Since this little guy hasn't been weaned yet, he needs to be with his mom to survive."

Then I turned to Momcat and gave her some instructions: "Take your baby and bring it back under the deck."

She didn't need to be told twice. In a few swift movements, she untangled her kitten from the net. Picking him up by the back of his neck, she walked briskly down the stairs and disappeared behind the bushes.

"How did you know that she would understand that?" James asked.

"I didn't," I said, just as astonished as he was.

"Maybe you are a cat whisperer, Mommy!"

The whole family laughed, and Bill suggested that we make a celebratory breakfast. We spent the rest of the day talking about the morning's events. Needless to say, we were all were grateful that the crisis was over and were thrilled that it had a happy ending!

10

MEETING OUR NEW CAT FAMILY

Two weeks after the window well incident, the kittens were ready for their big debut. As was my usual routine, upon waking, I went over to the bedroom window that overlooked the backyard.

To my delight, that morning I saw five little kittens milling about the deck, exploring every nook and cranny they could find. Momcat stood off to the side, proudly watching over her offspring. Junior also kept an eye on the kittens (from the sidelines) while sprawled out in his favorite spot at the far edge of the deck. Every so often, I could hear the kittens' faint, squeaky voices as they stumbled over one another while trying to steady their land legs.

Unable to contain my excitement any longer, I ran to wake up the rest of the family. Together, we all filed down the stairs and out to the deck.

As soon as we opened the back door, the kittens scrambled over to huddle around our feet. There were also one or two attempts to climb up John and James' legs! Meanwhile, Momcat glanced boastfully in our direction as if to say: *Here they are! This is my family!*

Although Momcat seemed comfortable with the initial interaction, I was a little nervous about how she would feel if we picked up one of her babies. Honestly, I had *no idea* what the proper protocol was in this situation. But before I could deliberate on the matter further, I saw that the boys each had a kitty in hand. The ones remaining on the ground darted in and out and around their legs. I glanced back at Momcat, who didn't even bat an eye. In fact, she seemed grateful for the mini hiatus after six weeks of looking after these little hoodlums.

We spent the rest of the morning playing with the kittens and letting them crawl all over us. Not even Bill could resist their cuteness! Within moments of venturing out onto the deck, we could see that he, too, was smitten with the kittens. There was no denying it.

Seven cats! What a responsibility our family now has! I thought, while watching the flurry of activity.

Momcat must have been nursing still because as soon as she laid down, all the kittens scampered over and lined up at her tummy. However, I figured that she would be weaning them soon, so it was only a matter of time before their meals would become *my* responsibility. This meant that I had to make *another* trip to the pet store to restock on kibble. So, with everyone preoccupied with the kitties, I excused myself and went back inside to get ready.

THE PET store owner was amused to see me again. He couldn't help but laugh when I told him that the two tabbies that adopted us had now multiplied into a seven-member family.

"I'm so intrigued by this whole story," he said. "You should really write a book about it someday!"

I chuckled at the idea, then returned to the task at hand.

After a brief consultation, I walked out of there with a variety of food for our newly expanded family. Between the adult chow for Momcat and Junior and the fodder for the kittens, the tabbies would soon have access to an *all-they-could-eat* buffet.

Of course, in the weeks that followed, I had a hard time

keeping everyone fed. It seemed that these kittens were *constantly* hungry, which puzzled me since they had such tiny tummies. *Where did they put it all?!* But this laborious feeding routine also gave me a lot of time to get to know the youngsters and observe their everyday shenanigans.

It seemed like the entire cat family consisted of early risers. I, too, liked to wake up before the rest of the world. This meant getting to watch Momcat and Junior nudge the herd of little ones up the steps of the deck for their breakfast.

Despite their small size, each kitten was able to clumsily climb from the grass to the deck, one stair at a time. From there, they all proceeded to trot proudly over to their food bowls.

One after the other, every kitten celebrated this modest accomplishment by adding a little swagger to its step. It was adorable to watch the ritual play out.

After breakfast, a flurry of playful activities would commence. Among the most amusing was the way the kittens interacted with the doghouse that I had purchased for their mother and half-brother earlier that year.

Next to the doghouse were two dirt-packed planters, which the toddlers soon took a liking to. The three orange-striped kittens would pile into one, while the two beige kittens settled into the other.

For children of any age, however, sitting around becomes boring after a while. It didn't take long before they began leaping from the planters to the roof of the doghouse.

To my dismay, the kittens followed in the footsteps of their caretakers — meaning that they had zero interest in venturing *into* this plastic structure, yet an unexplained enthusiasm for perching themselves *on top of it*. But with five kittens, there wasn't enough room for everyone to be up there at the same time. Thus, it fell upon the first kitten that made it to the top to shove the others off the roof, KING-OF-THE-HILL style. The whole clan seemed to love this game and often used it to entertain themselves for hours.

One of their other favorite activities was to empty out their water bowl as fast as possible. This was done for the sole purpose of using it for a pick-up game of soccer. If one of the kittens swung at the bowl hard enough, it would skid across the deck. This, in turn, led the rest of the kittens to chase after it. Then the next little hooligan would take a swipe at it and the game would continue.

After they had exhausted themselves, the kittens would pile up on top of their mother and treat themselves to a long afternoon nap. But post-nap? That was the time to continue the escapades...with none other than their Uncle Junior.

Usually, by late afternoon, Junior was ready to wander into the woods and do a little hunting. Meanwhile, the kittens liked to take this opportunity to stalk their half-brother into the yard. This was done despite knowing that they were *strictly forbidden* to leave the deck. What they didn't know was that Junior had appointed himself THE ENFORCER of this rule.

The moment any of the kittens set a single paw in the grass, he would come racing over, screeching his disapproval. It was like he had eyes in the back of his head!

Once he was face-to-face with the delinquent kitty, he would pick it up by the back of its neck and fling it up on the deck. This was followed by further disciplinary screeching to *stay put*, which the kittens would quickly dismiss before regrouping to plot their next round of antics.

As children do, Momcat's tribe of troublemakers got a kick out of testing Junior's patience, again and again, but never made it very far. The game was KITTENS VS. JUNIOR, and boy, did they love to play it!

After dinner, the family would retire to their quarters below the deck. Both Momcat and Junior seemed to agree that adhering to a strict PUT-THE-KIDS-TO-BED-EARLY policy was best for everyone. And so it would be for the rest of the summer.

11

THE STANDOFF

B y this time, summer was in full swing! Both John and James
were thrilled to be done with another school year. As for
the kittens, they showed just as much enthusiasm at having the
boys around during the day. Between the Downey children and
the tabby younglings, our deck was bustling with life. Together,
they spent those hot summer days chasing one another and
climbing on anything they could find.

With her offspring in good hands, Momcat would often go
for a walk in the yard and sun herself in the grass, away from all
the commotion. Junior also used the opportunity to get some
alone time. He continued to disappear into the woods for hours,
most likely to do a little hunting or harass some poor creature.
Not wanting to miss a meal, however, he *always* made sure to be
back for dinner.

One night, after John and James had gone to bed, Bill and I
heard a great deal of excitement out on the deck. At first, the
hissing noises sounded like they were coming from Junior —
something I hadn't heard since the night he confronted the
opossum. Suddenly, Momcat joined in. That's when I knew the
situation had to be quite serious.

"Oh no, here we go *again,*" I groaned, knowing all too well that there must be another animal trying to loot the kitten's food bowl.

Since Momcat had stopped nursing, I decided to reopen the all-night diner...so that the babies wouldn't go hungry during the night. Now I was beginning to regret that decision.

"We better check it out and make sure that everyone is okay," Bill said.

I nodded in agreement, and we both made our way over to the porch door to switch on the outside lights.

There was Junior, standing in attack position and ready to fight yet another opossum. Momcat stood next to him, creating a protective barrier between the intruder and her kittens. (Despite staying as close to safety as possible, it was clear that, like us, they also wanted to witness the action that was about to unfold.)

Bill was ready to go out and intervene when Junior decided to make his move. Just like the last time, all it took was a single THWAP! of his paw and the opossum scurried off towards the woods. As quickly as the confrontation had escalated, it had been resolved. *Crisis averted.*

With that, the cat family called it a night and headed back to bed.

———

A FEW DAYS after the opossum incident, Junior didn't show up for breakfast. He rarely missed a meal, which was our first indication that something was wrong.

It wasn't until later that afternoon — when John and James were outside playing with the kittens — that he came up on the deck. Right away, the boys called for me.

"MOM! Come out here! Junior's hurt!" John shouted.

I went out to see what was wrong. That's when I noticed that he had both a limp and a gash over his left eye.

"What do you think happened to him?" James asked.

"I don't know, but, knowing Junior, he probably got into a

fight with another animal," I said, crouching down to get a better look.

"We should take him to the doctor though, to make sure that this cut doesn't get infected. Would you boys mind fetching the cat box?"

In no time at all, we managed to lift Junior into the box and wedge it into the middle of the backseat. James and John sat down on either side of Junior and did anything they could to make him comfortable.

Even though he didn't appear to be in any agony, Junior certainly wasn't himself. This made for a very mellow car ride over to the vet, compared to the last road trip we had taken together. There were no meows or desperate attempts to escape. He just laid there on his side and quietly waited for us to reach our destination.

When we arrived at the clinic, I brought Junior inside, with the boys following close behind.

The doctor took a few minutes to shave off some fur around the injured eye before stitching up the cut and placing a cone around Junior's neck. To my surprise, Junior laid there and tolerated this invasion of his personal space. After giving him a quick shot to ward off any possible infection, the veterinarian took a few minutes to examine Junior's injured leg.

"It's just a bruise," he reassured me. "But it's good that you brought him in."

"Will he be okay?" James asked.

"Oh, he'll be fine. He just needs to go home and rest for a few days," the vet replied.

"Be sure to keep the cut clean and bring him back here next week. I'll remove the stitches then."

"Thank you, doctor. We'll be sure to do that."

With that, we all piled back into the car and headed home. Along the way, I couldn't help chuckling to myself.

Just when things feel like they are getting back to normal, something new comes up. We can't seem to catch a break with these tabbies!

That's when James brought up something that had crossed all of our minds: "Wait 'til Daddy hears about this one!"

We all burst out laughing, knowing that Bill would take one look at Junior and ask his favorite question: "How much did this free cat cost me today?"

JUNIOR TAKES ON NEW
RESPONSIBILITIES

Poor Junior. Seven days with a plastic cone around his neck might as well have been an eternity. He couldn't itch his stitched-up eye nor properly bathe himself, which, of course, irritated him to no end. His days were now spent sleeping on the deck, with all hunting activities halted until further notice. It didn't take a rocket scientist to see that he was bored out of his mind.

On the bright side, the kittens seemed to understand that Uncle Junior wasn't himself and took a break from their usual teasing and taunting. This gave him lots of space to heal and rest.

One week later, the long wait was over. Those pesky stitches came out and the cone was tossed in the garbage can. Our beloved Junior was back to being his typical invincible self. Sadly, however, this would be short-lived...as life had other plans for the cat family.

Less than a month after Junior's recovery, I saw the kittens make their way up the stairs to the deck, alongside Junior. Momcat, on the other hand, was noticeably absent. *That's odd,* I thought, trying not to worry. But in my heart, I knew that something was not right. Momcat hadn't let the kittens out of her sight since the birth, and she wouldn't have abandoned them, especially at this age. *So, where on earth could she be?*

The hours ticked by slowly that day as we waited for her to show up. The boys grew increasingly concerned, as did I, with each passing minute feeling like an eternity.

I replayed the previous night's events in my mind, trying to recall whether Momcat had behaved differently, or if I had seen her wander out of the yard after dark. Yet my last interaction with her had been nothing but ordinary. She had eaten her dinner, along with the rest of the kittens, then ushered everyone under the deck, as was her normal routine. I didn't remember seeing her after that.

Could she have ventured into the woods after putting her little ones to bed? Was she attacked by an animal? Could she be stranded out there, wounded or crying for help?

These thoughts soon gave way to even darker ones.

We don't live too far from the main road...what if she walked into the street and got hit by a car?

The longer I thought about it, the more I could feel my heart sink deeper into my chest. By that afternoon, I couldn't bear to sit around any longer. *Something had to be done.*

"Boys, I feel like something prevented Momcat from returning home to her babies. I think we should go search for her."

"I think so too," James agreed.

"We can make flyers and put them up around town!" said John.

"Sounds good. How about you and Dad work on those, while James and I ask the neighbors if they have seen her?"

"Okay."

The game plan was to divide and conquer. I wasn't optimistic that our efforts would turn up anything, but I could see that it was lifting the family's spirits. Surely, doing something was better than sitting around and doing nothing. So, without further deliberation, John and Bill focused on putting together some flyers, while James and I made our way out to the street.

We went from door-to-door, asking if anyone had seen our beautiful, marmalade-colored tabby. *No one had.*

So, we hopped in the car and began to drive around the neighborhood, calling out for Momcat. *Still no sign of her.*

By the time we returned home, Bill and John had finished making the flyers that alerted everyone to our missing cat. Together with James, they placed the flyers in mailboxes, pinned them up on light posts, and handed them out to local businesses. Meanwhile, I stayed at the house, in case she showed up.

DAYS WENT BY, and Momcat did not return. No one ever called to say that they had seen her, and her little body never turned up. To this day, we still don't know what happened; and because of that, there has never been any real closure.

For weeks after Momcat's disappearance, I struggled with the sadness of it all. My mind kept drifting back to the first day she showed up on our deck, greeting me with all the warmth and affection of a long-lost friend. I realized that having a pet — whether it's a cat or a dog or some other animal — always ends with such sadness. Pets just don't live as long as humans do, which is a difficult fact to face at the end of the day.

The only positive thing to come out of any of this was the change that took place in Junior's demeanor. Overnight, his role shifted from deputy caretaker to the primary custodian of the five little kittens. Without missing a beat, he made the transition seamlessly. It was so seamless, in fact, that his young counter-parts didn't appear to notice this major change in circumstance. It was amazing to witness.

From that day forward, I never saw Junior leave the yard. His focus shifted towards attending to the kittens' needs and also maintaining discipline among them. To our surprise, he even allowed all five siblings to snuggle against his belly — as though they were nursing — whenever he stretched out for his after-noon nap. I couldn't believe my eyes the first time I saw it!

It wasn't all fun and games, however. Junior took his new responsibilities *very* seriously, which meant that the time had come to teach the kittens to fend for themselves.

Now it was time for JUNIOR'S SCHOOL.

13

JUNIOR'S SCHOOL

The one thing that hadn't changed since Momcat's disappearance was the strict NO-LEAVING-THE-DECK rule. This was something that Junior continued to enforce with great enthusiasm. Yet, not a day went by where the kittens passed up the opportunity to test their new guardian. All it took was a casual paw off the deck stairs and a quick, over-the-shoulder glance back to see whether he had noticed.

One could argue that the kittens occasionally suffered from a lapse of memory and were eager to follow Junior as he prowled around in the grass. After all, kittens like to have fun too!

Memory lapse or not, Junior made no exceptions. A shrill MEOW! would come flying out of his mouth the very second he noticed a kitten fugitive prancing about the yard. This was then followed by a quick sprint over to the rule-breaker to pick it up (roughly, I might add) by the neck and toss it back on the deck. For extra measure, Junior would reprimand the kitten with a fierce tongue lashing until order had been restored.

As time went on, it was clear that the kittens were growing restless and needed something to keep themselves busy. Junior knew just the remedy and ventured into the woods first thing one morning to fetch a mouse.

At first, we all thought that he had returned to hunting for sport and exercise. However, when he came back with a live, squirming vermin in his mouth, we realized that it was a form of training for the kittens.

This was the beginning of MOUSING IOI.

Upon his return, Junior dropped the mouse on the deck, keeping it in place with one of his giant paws. Then he proceeded to instruct each kitten to line up, side-by-side, in an orderly fashion. The younglings stood at attention, waiting for their next set of instructions. *Now, class could begin.*

In one fell swoop, Junior tossed the mouse into the air and batted it around. It was a lot like a game of HOT POTATO. Meanwhile, the kittens watched closely, eager for a chance to play with the mouse too.

When the small creature finally hit the deck, it ran for its life. Junior followed close behind, and the kittens chased after him. Seconds later, the mouse was once again held captive by one of Junior's paws, and he screeched at the kittens to fall back in line. They, of course, complied with these orders. In return, Junior rewarded the student closest to him by placing the mouse in front of it. Now the kitten had to demonstrate what it had just learned.

The largest member of the pack took the lead and executed the release and recapture of the rodent with an impressive amount of skill and tact. One after the other, each sibling came to the head of the class to illustrate its understanding of the lesson. Everyone seemed eager to get a nod of approval from their teacher. (To my relief, no one tried to kill nor eat the mouse, but the poor thing certainly underwent enough torture.)

Finally, the family of cats had enough playtime with their living toy and allowed it to seek refuge in some nearby bushes.

What amazed me about this sequence of events was how much they resembled a school for humans. I swear, if Junior had had a ruler and could speak English, he would have said, "Okay, pay attention. Here's the mouse and this is what you do: *Throw it up in the air. Use your paws to bat it this way, then that way. Let it run a bit, so it thinks it is home-free. Then, you pounce!*"

Yet, his demonstrations were so clear that no words were necessary.

The kittens, for their part, played their role as students perfectly. They were attentive, patient, and completed this assignment using their natural instincts. To this day, I'm still impressed when I think back on it. Without question, Junior was an excellent instructor. That said, I am sure the kittens listened, in part, because they feared the consequences of not following THE ENFORCER's rules. It was a tough love approach, and an effective one at that.

MOUSING 101 was a great success, but there were other life skills that the kittens still needed to learn. Next up on the list? *Tree climbing!*

Adjacent to the deck was a beautiful crab apple tree, which provided the ideal setting for Junior's climbing lessons. Once again, the kittens lined up, sat poised on their little rumps, and gave him the spotlight. This time, however, they were allowed to come down from the deck and observe from the grassy area beneath the tree.

Junior showed the kittens what to do by going up the tree and down the tree, then up again and down again. On the way up, he would extend his claws, dig into the bark, and use his limbs to hug the tree and swiftly work his way up to the first branches. On the way down, he took a similar approach but went butt-first rather than head-first, which I assumed was his way of reducing the risk of falling.

The entire journey — six feet each way — was very calculated and methodical. During this time, the kitties' eyes and heads moved up and down in unison with Junior's body, as though they were watching a ball being tossed back and forth.

Now it was time for each member of the group to attempt a solo climb. If the task was completed successfully, they passed the class. If not, they would have to try again. Junior encouraged each kitten, one after another, by nudging them forward with his nose. Those that remained on the ground were quiet and still, anxious to undertake this harrowing task.

I held my breath in anticipation as the first one bravely demonstrated its tree climbing ability. Fortunately, it succeeded the first time around with no intervention on my part nor Junior's. The second one also passed with flying colors, as did the last two. KITTEN #3, however, made it up to the branches, took one look at the ground below and froze in its tracks. Frightened, it began to cry out for help. Junior immediately came to the rescue.

Up he went to grab the stranded pupil by the back of its neck and carry it down to safety. After the kitten had a minute to calm down, Junior encouraged it to try again with another little nudge.

This time, the climb went flawlessly, with KITTEN #3 inching its way up the tree and scooting back down again. Meanwhile, its instructor remained on standby to ensure that his family member stayed safe.

Now that the kittens were all accomplished tree climbers and knew how to hunt for food, Junior eased up on his strict rules. As for his other lessons, they were worked into the kittens' daily activities. These teaching opportunities were less structured but more frequent and focused mostly on self-defense. This was essential for any grown-up cat, and it was Junior's favorite lesson of them all.

To work in the element of surprise, he would wait until the kittens were fully immersed in playtime before rushing across the deck and pouncing on them. The gang of kittens teamed up and pounced back, but they were no match for Junior's size. From there, he would wrestle each youngster and bat them around, just as he had done with the mouse.

Admittedly, I wasn't a fan of all the rough housing that went on and often felt the need to intervene. Junior seemed to find this amusing and dismissed my scolding by turning his back to me. *Clearly, no one was going to get in the way of* JUNIOR'S SCHOOL.

14

LET SLEEPING RACCOONS SLEEP

Junior's lessons in self-defense were put to the test a week later.

It was the middle of the afternoon when I first heard the shrieks. These were not Junior's usual shrill *meows*, however. These were terrified cries for help!

Looking out the kitchen window, I saw him running for his life towards the deck. His ears were flattened against his head and a look of fear was plastered across his face. Following close behind was the fattest raccoon I had ever seen in my life...*and he was furious.* Without a doubt, Junior was in serious trouble.

I knew that raccoons were nocturnal, so it was startling to see this one out in broad daylight. Months before, I had noticed it moved into the same tree hole where the kittens had been born. Because of the tree's proximity to the backyard, I figured that Junior must have taunted and pestered the creature to no end. Obviously, the raccoon had had enough of these antics and was ready to retaliate. Whatever the final straw I'll never know for sure, but it didn't take a genius to see what was coming next. This animal wanted revenge. And if he caught Junior, it would *not* end well.

Suddenly, I remembered that the kittens were playing up on the deck. I worried if I didn't go out and defend them, the raccoon would make a meal out of them. *Five bites and they'd be gone!*

Since Bill had taken the boys to the movies that day, I was on my own to deal with the situation. I'll be honest, the idea of facing that raccoon alone was *terrifying*.

As the impending battle closed in on the deck, I had no choice but to run outside and stand in front of the kittens, making sure to close the door behind me. *If worse comes to worst, I'll shove them inside,* I reassured myself.

The minute the tabbies saw Junior and the lumbering raccoon coming towards the deck, they went on high alert and huddled together.

Around this time, I realized that I needed some kind of weapon to defend all of us. Frantic, I scanned the deck for something I could use. Luckily, there was a broom within arm's reach. I grabbed it and held on for dear life. *This was going to get ugly.*

A split-second later, the two rivals had made their way up the steps. I positioned myself, in full power stance, in front of the kittens to protect them...not realizing that Junior wanted protection too.

In no time at all, he had gone from MACHO MAN to SCAREDY-CAT, and quickly ducked behind both me and the kittens. *Great.*

Now there was nothing standing between me and the raccoon. Worried that he might try to go after me to get to Junior — or worse, the kittens — I began to advance on the angry creature. I shouted and whooped at him as loud as I could, fiercely swinging the broom in front of me and stomping my feet to scare him off. (I'm sure I looked like a crazy lady.) Meanwhile, the kittens and Junior remained frozen in place, making no effort to help.

I was afraid to turn my back, even for a second, so I kept moving towards the raccoon to try to run him off. In response to my banshee-like shrieking and intense broom-swatting, he stopped in his tracks and watched me.

The ugly standoff felt like hours, but probably lasted only a few minutes before the raccoon decided to retreat. His pursuit of Junior simply wasn't worth the effort anymore, now that a human was involved. But despite giving up, he didn't seem at all rattled nor did he give off an air of defeat, perhaps to save face.

Once I saw him climb the tree and disappear into his little dwelling, I turned my attention to Junior and was absolutely *livid.*

"*You* caused this, Junior! You put *everyone* in danger, including *me*! If I hadn't been here, you would've been dinner! As would your brothers and sisters! Don't you *ever* go near that tree again!" I shouted.

He seemed to understand that he had crossed a line and walked over to make amends. The kittens, on the other hand, stayed put and didn't move a muscle. I'm sure they didn't know what was more frightening: the vengeful raccoon or this infuriated woman. It wasn't until I sat down, and Junior climbed into my lap, that they understood the coast was clear and the crisis had been averted.

I spent the rest of the day outside with them, worried that if I left, even for a moment, the raccoon would return to exact his revenge.

Junior was still shaken up and stuck by me the whole time. I knew at that moment that I would never have to lecture him on taunting raccoons again. After all, everyone knows that it's best to let sleeping raccoons *sleep.*

15

RAISING THE KITTENS ON OUR OWN

R aising five kittens was never the life Junior wanted. The responsibility defaulted to him after Momcat's disappearance, and he fulfilled his duties faithfully. However, his patience began to wane after a month of teaching his siblings the necessary skills to survive in the wild. And it didn't take long before the desire for a life of freedom returned.

Junior began spending an increasing amount of time away from the house, and the kittens, often not returning at night. That's when we all knew that his time with us was coming to its natural end. Now, it was a matter of waiting for the right opportunity to leave his siblings once and for all, so that he could go and start a life of his own.

To my surprise, the kittens didn't appear to mind Junior's absence...even as it grew from hours to days at a time. In fact, they seemed to adapt quite well to the changing situation.

As more time passed, the tribe of siblings grew more self-reliant. Of course, they still stuck together, playing on the deck during the day and sleeping under it at night. At two and a half months old, they also never left the deck, even when it was obvious that THE ENFORCER was on the verge of moving on. *(Clearly, his training had been effective!)*

After a week or so of "testing the waters" to see how the

kitties would fare without him, Junior finally made up his mind to leave — this time for good. It took about another week before we were sure that we would never see him again.

He no longer came back to the house for mealtimes.

He didn't seek refuge beneath the deck at night.

He never again ran to us for help if he got into any trouble.

This was it. Junior had moved on.

In all honesty, none of us was that torn up about his leaving the family. From the first day he showed up at our door, he had never given anyone the chance to truly bond with him. And that was okay. Between his anti-social personality and the distance he maintained from the rest of us, it was difficult to connect with him. I always thought of Junior as a strange fellow, but he was who he was, and I accepted that fact early on.

Neither Bill nor I nor the boys thought that something bad had happened to Junior. He may not have said a proper goodbye, but he gave us enough notice by easing out of his role as a guardian. Ultimately, it was Junior's decision. Knowing him, I'm sure he felt that he had stayed long enough.

Without Momcat and Junior around, it was time to get more realistic about caring for the five kittens on my own. I worried about their sleeping arrangements beneath the deck and how exposed they were to hungry animals. I was also concerned about their exposure to the elements, especially since the Midwest can have severe thunderstorms during the summer and bone-chilling cold winters.

When it came to these matters, there was only so much I could do to protect them, considering that I couldn't bring them indoors. The most rational solution was growing more and more obvious: *Soon enough, we would have to let some of the tabbies go.*

———

As HAPPENS WITH ALL PETS, the kittens were developing person-alities of their own. Thus, it was time to give them names based on their most distinctive traits. Among the three orange tabbies

— who were almost identical — the boys and I decided on
FRIENDLY, TIGGER, and MARMALADE.

Friendly had inherited his mother's warm and loving
temperament.

Tigger had large paws just like a tiger.

Marmalade had a beautiful marmalade-colored coat.

As for the two beige kitties, we chose the names PRINCESS
and PANDORA, as they were both very regal and dignified. They
often separated themselves from the rest of the group and maintained a sense of propriety when it came to the usual rough and
tumble of playtime.

Now that we had named them, it was time to take a quick
visit to the vet for checkups and vaccinations. Of course, as with
Momcat and Junior, none of these kittens had been confined
indoors before, let alone the inside of a car. And if I thought
that traveling with two cats was a challenge, taking a trip with
five was going to be a *true* test of sanity! So, I enlisted John and
James to assist in the endeavor.

Together, we loaded the kittens, one by one, into our cardboard cat carrier. To sweeten the deal, I threw in a can of tuna.

Initially, the whole gang seemed to think of the box as a
grand adventure. However, as soon as we closed the top and
loaded them into the car, claustrophobia kicked in and mayhem
descended. High-pitched cries and squeaky meows could be
heard coming from each and every window and air hole.

Then, the escape attempts took over, with little arms and
noses desperately jammed through the tiny openings. It was as if
they were sure they could squeeze and contort their little bodies
through the one-inch windows. Their constant scrambling and
scratching, whining and begging, was almost deafening. Needless
to say, the kittens were *not* happy about their temporary incar-
ceration.

James and John sat on either side of the box and did what
they could to control the situation. In an attempt to comfort the
distraught kittens, they opened the top flaps to give everyone
some extra breathing room. Two of the angrier siblings managed

to catapult themselves out of the box and into John's lap but settled down shortly after that. The others tried to climb out as well but were unsuccessful.

Thankfully, the car ride was over in a matter of minutes. Upon our arrival, the three of us hauled the box of kittens into the waiting room, which appeared to be quiet and orderly...until we showed up.

Additional escape attempts were made as the cats worked in unison to rock the box, back and forth, until it tipped over and the top broke open. Then it was a game of CATCH-ME-IF-YOU-CAN to gather up the hooligans and usher their little bee-hinds into the examination room.

Despite all the chaos, the vet remained in good humor and welcomed us with an amused smirk.

"Finally, I get to meet the rest of the cat family!" he said.

"Yes, here they are." I replied, laughing.

"Now, which one of you is the kitten that fell into the window well?"

"That would be Friendly," I said, pointing toward the only chill cat in the group.

Meanwhile, the rest were wandering about the room, exploring every nook and cranny as Junior had done during his first visit.

"I'll check him out first then," the vet replied, picking Friendly up and placing him on the exam table.

After some poking and prodding, Friendly received his shots and was sent on his way.

The remaining checkups went just as smoothly. The kittens were well-behaved, for the most part, and allowed the doctor to do what needed to be done. (*Although it was clear that none of them cared much for this strange man and his cold metal table.*)

By the end, all were pronounced healthy and free of worms, fleas, and ticks. This announcement came as a relief to me, as I was sure they had caught something during their months of outdoor life.

"How are the other two cats doing?" the vet asked, as the boys and I gathered up the kittens for the ride home.

"Well, Momcat disappeared about a month ago. We don't know exactly what happened to her, but we suspect that she may have been hit by a car. As for Junior, he decided that being a parent wasn't for him and left us about a week ago."

"I'm sorry to hear that."

"Thank you. But we have made our peace with it, and the kittens seem to be doing fine on their own."

"I couldn't agree more," he replied with a smile.

With that, it was time to make our way back to the house.

———

ARRIVING AT HOME, the boys and I hauled the cat carrier out of the car and back to the deck. From there, we tipped the box on its side and let the kittens roam freely. Boy, were they thrilled!

Within minutes, the whole tribe was back to their usual antics. All the commotion caused Bill to come out and join the party.

"How did the trip to the vet go?" he asked.

"Oh, it was fine. Everything was normal, and they got their shots."

"These free cats are costing more money each day, it seems. But I'll admit, they are quite cute," he said with a chuckle.

A short pause followed before he brought up his next concern.

"You're not going to neuter and spay them, are you?"

"Oh god, no!" I replied, then lowered my voice so the boys couldn't hear.

"We need to start finding homes for them soon. Having five kittens is just too much, and I worry that something might happen to them if they remain under the deck."

Bill agreed, and the plan was set into motion.

16

MOM OR THE KITTENS

The first step in finding the kittens a new home was to hold a family meeting and discuss the situation.

"You know, boys, now that summer is coming to an end, it's going to start getting cold outside. And I'm worried about the kitties now that Junior isn't around. They don't have much protection under the deck, and that raccoon might come back, at some point, looking for a snack or a full meal. That is why your dad and I think that we should find the kittens a new home, where they'll be out of harm's way."

John and James weren't too happy about my proposal and were adamant that a preliminary vote be taken. This would determine whether the family would keep all of the kittens or find a new home for *me*, the mother! After all, it was *my* severe allergies to cats that were the issue here.

"Couldn't you just find another place to live, Mommy?" James asked.

"Yeah!" John chimed in. "If you moved out, the kittens could live inside our house, where it's cozy and warm."

That's when I reminded the boys that I was the one who packed their lunches, kept the house clean, made dinner at night, and read them bedtime stories. This gave them pause and made them reconsider their initial proposal. Thus, a second vote was called for.

This time around, it was declared that I would remain with the family, and we would find homes for three of the kittens. The whole family agreed; this was a reasonable compromise.

As for the kittens that would be given away, we decided that the girls should be the ones to go. We simply hadn't bonded with them as much as Tigger and Friendly. This included the two beige ones, Princess and Pandora, as well as Marmalade, who shared the same orange stripes as her brothers. Meanwhile, the boy tabbies would continue living with us but remain outdoors.

With everyone in agreement, the next step in the process was to find a new family for the kittens. Someone who could provide them with a safe and loving home.

This was the easy part, as I had been giving my coworkers regular updates on the feline family. One of them, a professor of history, was especially interested in the kittens and jumped at the chance to adopt the three females. He seemed particularly fond of the two beige ones, which was ideal since they were practically inseparable.

Because my colleague loved cats and was familiar with raising them, I felt that he would be a perfect match for Princess, Pandora, and Marmalade. He also lived on a small farm, which meant that the three girls would have lots of room to roam and play — away from busy roads and wooded areas filled with opossums and raccoons.

As an added measure, I interviewed this coworker, at length. *(After all, these cats were like children to me!)* I also wanted to be sure that he knew what he was getting. I mentioned that the girls were outdoor cats, although they could, in theory, be domesticated. They didn't bite or scratch. They weren't spayed but had their required vaccinations. This information seemed to go over well, and the interview ended with a resounding, "Yes, I will take all three!"

Now, all that remained was to transport the kittens up to the college for the hand-off. However, unlike our earlier road trips, this car ride would take around 40 minutes or so, depending on traffic. And since the boys were finishing up their last week of summer camp, I would be on my own during the drive. *This,* I told myself, *is going to be quite the adventure.*

The next day, I loaded the homemade cat carrier, along with the three girls, into the backseat. Then I mentally prepared myself for the long day ahead. Fortunately, the drive consisted of back roads, so I crossed my fingers that very few cars would be around. With everyone situated, we were on our way!

Of course, the first five minutes were filled with deafening meows and protests. I resisted the temptation to comfort them and soldiered on. Shortly thereafter, the three kittens began to rock their box until it tipped on its side and the top flew open. Then out they ran, all the detainees, eager to explore their strange surroundings.

Marmalade, however, was still trapped inside. She had somehow managed to get her paw stuck in one of the window cutouts and was unable to free herself. I eventually had to pull over and tend to the situation. While I was at it, I decided to load the other two kittens back into the box and secure the top once again, for safety reasons. Then I hopped back in the driver's seat, and we continued to make our way up to the college campus.

Everything seemed fine for the next few minutes. In fact, the kittens didn't make a sound. *That's odd,* I thought. *Maybe they are getting used to the box.*

Just then, I felt a little paw on my right shoulder. I glanced in the rearview mirror and saw Marmalade perched on the edge of the driver's seat, perfectly content with taking in the view ahead. Princess and Pandora had also found the perfect spot, in the very back, to sit on their hind legs and watch the cars pass.

Initially, I was afraid that they would be running all over the car and cause an accident. My fear, however, turned out to be unfounded. Given how content they were, I decided to leave them be. So, with Marmalade as my co-driver, we finished out the road trip in peace and without any other hiccups.

THE PROFESSOR and I had agreed to meet in one of the campus parking lots before class. When I pulled up, I saw that he had a pick-up truck and offered to lend him my box for the kittens.

"No, that's alright. I'll just put them in the cab and let them wander around. I think they will be happier with that," he replied, gesturing toward the three little sisters climbing all over the back of my car.

I laughed and agreed with him. *Who knew? If I had just let the cats roam around freely, it would have solved all my transport problems from the beginning.*

In any case, it was now time to say goodbye to my adopted children and hand them over to their new caretaker. One by one, I passed them off to the professor and watched as he placed them in his truck. Then I thanked him for giving the kittens a new home and headed over to my office.

Driving away felt bittersweet, but I also felt relieved. It was difficult to see the kittens go, but I knew that they would be safer at the professor's farm than on the back deck of our house. Plus, they had each other.

Now we were down to just two tabbies.

17

ONLY TWO REMAIN

In the weeks that followed, Friendly and Tigger seemed to adjust just fine to life without their sisters. As in the past, they continued to sleep beneath the deck at night and play up top during the day. They took their afternoon naps in the dirt-filled planters and climbed onto the roof of the doghouse when they needed more amusement. After all, there was such a great view from the top!

By now, it was the end of September and the seasons were beginning to change. The weather turned cooler and autumn storms were now underway. One afternoon, while I was at work, a heavy rain started to fall. Minutes later, a strong wind picked up and that rain soon turned into hail.

Looking out the window, I thought about the two kittens and how cold and wet they must be, perhaps even frightened. To make matters worse, they had no adult supervision.

As with Momcat and Junior, I couldn't stand the thought of our adopted babies being in such an uncomfortable state. So, just as I had done the winter before, I made an executive decision to leave work early. That way, I could drive home and move the kittens into the garage.

On my way, I considered the logistics of moving the tabbies indoors. There was a possibility that they might try to run into the main part of the house or get run over by a car. I was also sure that I would never hear the end of this from my husband. But rather than worry about things that had yet to happen, I told myself that I would figure it out later. Right now, my kitties needed a proper shelter from the elements, and the garage was just right for the job.

Upon my arrival, I went out to the deck to find both Friendly and Tigger crouched beneath a nearby wooden bench — their only place of refuge from this awful autumn monsoon.

Seeing the miserable look on their faces nearly broke my heart. I ran out and scooped them both up — one cat under each arm — then sprinted into the garage. After setting them down, I ran back out to the deck to fetch the doghouse and bring that inside too. I thought the kittens would fare better if they had some remnant of their former life outdoors.

Both tabbies appeared to love exploring their new space, especially since there were so many interesting things to crawl around on! They also had lots of shelving to wander in and out of, as well as several other hidden corners to peruse. Needless to say, Tigger and Friendly were feeling very much at home here.

As for the doghouse, I placed it on Bill's tool bench, which was just over waist high. It took some maneuvering, but I managed to lift the bulky structure up there. Then I secured it so that it wouldn't topple over and crush anyone. I figured that the kittens could use it as an overlook for their new home turf.

During this time, I also scanned the area for anything that Friendly and Tigger might injure themselves on. For instance, a pair of scissors and a nearby hammer. I stashed these dangerous tools in a storage cabinet and proceeded to bring in their food and water bowls.

After the essentials were taken care of, I experienced a sudden moment of panic. *Oh my god. I need to get these cats a litter box or there'll be surprises everywhere!*

I also realized that since they had only ever used the great outdoors as their bathroom facility, I would have to introduce the kittens to the concept of a litter box. The prospect was daunting but necessary. Thus, it was off to the pet store yet again!

Fortunately, the owner of the store helped me find an appropriate box and a bag of kitty litter. And, after explaining the situation to him, he offered some advice on how to handle the training aspect of the endeavor.

"Just take both cats and place them in the litter box. They will know what to do from there."

I was a bit skeptical but went home and followed his recommendation to a T — placing the cats in the box and having a little chat with them.

"Alright kitties, you don't have the outdoors anymore, so this is what you have to use instead."

Friendly and Tigger stared at me for a moment and then walked around the litter box a few times before hopping out. *This is not going to work,* I thought and went inside the house to dry off from the rain.

When I came back, I was shocked to find that both tabbies had gone to the bathroom...*inside the litter box!* It was a miracle! After only one instruction, the kittens understood the purpose of this foreign object and used it accordingly. I was nothing short of amazed!

When John and James came home from school that day, they were thrilled to learn of the kittens' upgraded living arrangements. I, too, felt much better knowing that they were out of harm's way. Now, we just had to convince Bill that this was best for everyone.

As he pulled into the driveway, the boys and I ran out to warn him to use caution when entering the garage, so as not to run over the new tenants.

"What new tenants?" he asked.

"The kittens, Dad!" James shouted.

"We didn't want to leave them out in this terrible weather," I added.

Bill agreed that the kittens would be much better off in the garage than out on the deck...*for the night.* He then proceeded to drive in slowly so as not to disturb the little rascals. Now, all was right with the world.

WE WERE all curious to see how well the kitties had dealt with their first night in the garage. To our surprise (and amusement), we opened the door to find Friendly perched on top of my car and Tigger lounging on top of Bill's.

My husband, of course, was not as amused by this latest development and was impatient to leave for work. So, I gently removed Friendly from one car, while John reached up to grab Tigger from the other.

With both cats safely out of the way, Bill pulled out of the garage and headed down the driveway...only to turn around and come back minutes later. Confused, I walked outside to see what the problem was.

"Is everything okay?" I asked.

"Liz, do you see this?! There are paw prints all over my car and smear covering the front windshield!"

I inspected the car windows and saw what Bill was talking about. *The cats had had a field day!*

To remedy the situation, I grabbed some Windex and a cloth to wipe off the prints. After a quick polishing, my husband was back on the road again.

I decided to check my car as well, only to discover that my windshields were also smeared and covered in paw prints. This was perplexing, as none of us could figure out what the kittens were doing to create such a mess. So, the boys and I hatched a plan to investigate later that night. We were determined to solve this mystery together!

Our investigative work turned out to be even more amusing than the initial discovery. After some minutes observing the tabbies through the garage door window, we saw that our inventive kittens had made a game out of sliding down the slanted windows. Each one would work his way up one windshield and skid down the other, belly-first (or fanny-first.) And two cars meant that each one had his own slide to test out!

This was quite comical to watch, at least to me and the boys. Bill, however, did not find it as funny. In fact, he didn't like having the kittens in the garage at all because it made parking nearly impossible. He also didn't appreciate all the paw prints that were created in the kittens' quest to entertain themselves.

Friendly and Tigger felt the same way about the cars; they didn't like them in the garage. This was, in part, due to the loud, scary sounds made by the engines as well as the garage door. Hearing these sounds made both tabbies dodge behind the closest object for protection. They would then remain there on high alert until the coast was clear. Thus, the time had come to find a better solution.

18

NOW WE HAVE NO GARAGE

There was only one solution worth considering at this point: *The cars would have to be parked in the driveway, so that Friendly and Tigger could have the garage all to themselves.*

This made sense to the boys. It seemed logical to me. And it certainly would be met with approval by the kittens. However, none of this made any sense to Bill. He argued that the whole point of the garage was to keep the cars warm and dry. But since we didn't want to upset the kittens, parking the vehicles indoors was a convenience that he would have to live without.

Thus, from that day forward, the garage was controlled by the tabbies. *No car could enter. No car could exit.* In fact, the garage door was not to be used at all, as the cats didn't like the scary sounds it made.

To make matters worse, both Friendly and Tigger knew that the house was warmer than the garage and were always on the lookout for opportunities to dash inside. *(They were, undoubtedly, on a mission to create a better life for themselves.)*

John, James, and I found this more entertaining than anything else, but it seemed to create additional tension between Bill and the cats.

Everything came to a head the night that Bill and I had to attend a black-tie event in the city. We were both dressed to the nines. Bill in his tuxedo, and I in my evening gown and heels. Unfortunately, the weather did not cooperate with our plans that night and a sleet storm was well underway.

Because both vehicles were parked out in the driveway, we had no choice but to trudge through sleet and snow to reach them. The footpath to the driveway stretched the entire length of the house and was extremely slippery. This meant that Bill and I were sliding and stumbling down the path the whole way.

By the time we reached the door to the car, we were soaked from the sleet. I glanced over at my husband and saw that he was practically fuming.

"This is ridiculous! It's unacceptable! These free cats have completely taken over, and now we have no garage!"

Of course, I was in no position to say anything to the contrary. Bill was right; this arrangement was causing more problems than it solved.

The rest of the night, I found myself brainstorming alternative solutions to fix the situation. Ultimately, I came to the conclusion that, yet *another* kitten would have to go. As for the remaining tabby, he would have to learn to live with a fully functional garage. There was simply no other way.

19

IF THE GARAGE IS GOOD, THE
HOUSE MUST BE BETTER

K eeping the kittens out of the house was a constant battle. It didn't matter whether we were venturing into the garage for a visit or doing something as simple as taking the trash out.

Whenever the door connecting the house to the garage was opened, the kittens would bolt across the entryway. Then they would slide under the nearest piece of furniture — as if attempting to escape Alcatraz — and lay in wait for the "authorities" to give up their search.

Of course, encouraging them to come out was both difficult and time-consuming. And, all too soon, both Friendly and Tigger knew that life inside the house was, without a doubt, *far nicer* than life in the garage.

The whole escapade happened at least four or five times a day. While these escape attempts were an effective form of exercise, they were exhausting to say the least.

Eventually, the boys and I were able to corral the fugitives and escort them back to their quarters. Often times, however, the task of finding and retrieving the cats was left to me. (And holding one writhing tabby while trying to get a hold of the other proved to be quite the challenge!)

Sure, it made sense as to why the two brothers were so drawn to life inside the house. It was warmer than the garage and also more inviting. I also knew that they both wanted more time with John and James, who had become their favorite playmates beyond one another. But I could no longer justify the amount of time nor energy spent tracking down the kittens each day.

This is insane! I found myself thinking one afternoon. *I can't do this anymore.*

It had been only a week since the night Bill and I attended the black-tie event. Yet despite my earlier resolve, I hadn't been able to make a move on parting with another kitten just yet. After a few days of playing HIDE-AND-SEEK, however, I was more than ready to find one of the rascals a new home.

Another family meeting was held to discuss the future of the kittens and determine which would be the one to go. Friendly, of course, had endeared himself to us all. No one could bear the thought of parting with him. Tigger, however, had not bonded with any family member to the same extent. Thus, he was the obvious choice. The vote was unanimous: *It was time to begin the search for Tigger's new home.*

Fortunately, I knew that one of the nearby neighbors had taken an interest in Tigger specifically. She had heard the stories of Momcat and Junior from the very beginning and often inquired about how the litter of kittens was doing. She also lived by herself, so a feline companion would be a welcome addition. Figuring that she might still be interested, I gave her a call that night and let her know that one the younglings was available.

"Hello?"

"Hi Kathy, this is Liz from down the street. I wanted to let you know that we've decided to give away one of our kittens. Would you be interested in taking it?"

"Are you kidding? I'd be thrilled! Is it one of the orange-striped ones?

"It is! I hate to say it, but I'm eager to give this one away as soon as possible. He's well-behaved and has a great personality but taking care of these kittens has become too much, especially with my allergies."

"Don't worry, Liz. I would be happy to take him off your hands. I promise that he will be well looked after here."

"Thank you so much, Kathy. I really appreciate it. When can I bring him over?"

"Would tomorrow be too soon?"

"Tomorrow is perfect. I'll bring him by after work."

"Wonderful. See you then!"

"Bye Kathy. Thanks again."

Hanging up the phone, I felt a wave of relief wash over me. This was the best solution for our family, and I knew that Tigger would be happy in his new home.

The next day, I returned home from work, plucked Tigger from the garage and placed him under my arm. Together, we made our way down the street towards Kathy's place.

Tigger remained calm and seemed to enjoy being out in the fresh air again. His little nose twitched against the frosty October air, perhaps because he smelled the roast beef wafting over from one of the nearby houses.

This is much easier than the trip I had with the others, I mused. *He also doesn't seem to have any anxiety over being separated from his one remaining sibling.*

When we arrived, Kathy invited us in, and I set the curious tabby down on the carpeted floor. He then went off to explore the perimeter of the living room, checking every corner for God-knows-what. Meanwhile, I took the opportunity to go over a few things.

"Here," I said, giving her a piece of paper. "I wrote a few things down for you, which I hope will be helpful with Tigger. This is what we've been feeding him. He knows how to use a litter box. And as I mentioned on the phone, he's well-behaved but, of course, also loves to play."

"I think the two of us are going to get along just fine," Kathy replied, laughing.

"I think so too. See?" I said, pointing at Tigger, who was curled up on the coffee table. "He's already more at home here than he ever was in our garage."

With that, we said our goodbyes, and I began the return journey home. Life had become so crazy since the tabbies moved indoors and even before. Now, there was just one member of the cat family left.

I'll admit that I felt a huge burden lift off my shoulders, knowing that we were down to a single kitten. And even though it didn't completely solve the garage problem, it certainly made things easier.

FASTER THAN A SPEEDING BULLET

Now there was only one kitten: the infamous Friendly! Being both affectionate and cuddly by nature, this little guy had now become everyone's favorite tabby.

Whenever any of us gave in to his playful nudges for attention, we were rewarded with loud purrs that vibrated throughout his entire body. More often than not, the purring would become almost deafening. It grew so loud, in fact, that it sounded more like thunder than a delighted little kitty.

It was clear that Friendly dreamed of moving into the main part of the house. He knew that a better, more comfortable existence awaited him beyond the garage and was determined to have it.

I found it funny that Friendly had such a desire to live a domestic life, given that he had been born in a tree just months before. But, of course, this became his sole objective after Tigger moved out.

Like clockwork, the moment any of us opened the door to the garage, Friendly would make a break for it. He was like a speeding bullet — zooming through the laundry room to get to the rest of the house — where he could find some impossible-to-reach hiding spot.

One of his favorite places to hole up was under James' bed, which was up the stairs and at the end of the hallway. The bed frame was close to the floor and, thus, had very little clearance. Somehow, Friendly found a way to slither beneath it, always making his way to the very back (to avoid capture.)

After a few days of this, I decided to start closing the door connecting the laundry room to the rest of the house *before* opening the door to the garage. This didn't deter our resourceful little kitten, however. All he had to do now was find a new perch where none of us could reach him. Given the limited space he had to work with, there was only one viable option: the top of the laundry room cabinets.

If you ever saw the height of these cabinets, you would think that this was an unbelievable feat for a cat that was not yet fully grown. There were not many places to use as a launchpad, and the clearance from the top of the cabinets to the ceiling was only about six inches or so. Yet we saw Friendly perform this acrobatic trick many times.

It was accomplished by a quick sprint across the threshold of the entryway between the garage and the laundry room. This running start created enough momentum for him to take one enormous leap to the top of the washer, followed by yet another giant leap from the washer to the top of the cabinets.

How he managed to get into a huddle position just in time to clear the landing was nothing short of amazing. Friendly's combination of grace and precisely calculated jumps seemed to defy both the laws of gravity and the limits of athletic ability.

Upon successful execution of this skilled maneuver, he would curl up into a little ball and spend the rest of the afternoon watching over the laundry room.

I've often heard that animals don't have the ability to smile. However, the look on Friendly's face as he surveyed his new dominion was the closest thing to a smile that I had ever seen. Even though he couldn't talk, it was clear that he was trying to communicate his one true desire in life: *I want to be a house cat!*

Of all the places Friendly chose to hide or perch, the top of the laundry cabinets were, by far, the most difficult to reach. To retrieve him, I had to climb on top of the washer and reach up on my tiptoes to scoop him up.

Friendly, of course, hated this. He would meow in protest and scoot backwards until he was pressed against the wall — making it as excruciating as possible to get a hold of him.

Each time I had to escort our little friend back to the garage, a feeling of guilt would wash over me. I knew that Friendly felt lonely living out there by himself. Every attempt to escape further into the house was his way of pressuring me into letting him move indoors.

But Friendly wasn't the only one creating pressure; the boys were too. They wanted him to live inside the house just as much as he wanted to. Honestly, I wanted to let Friendly live in the house with us too, but I wasn't sure I would be able to keep my allergies at bay if I made that concession.

Since he seemed to enjoy the laundry room so much, I came to the conclusion that perhaps he could move in there. It was far enough away from the bedrooms and had tiled flooring, so the dander from his fur wouldn't build up enough to set off my allergies. It would also be easy to keep the door closed to prevent him from entering the rest of the house. *This just might work,* I thought. *And it will allow Bill to have his garage back.*

Once again, a family meeting was held to discuss Friendly's living arrangements. Right away, John and James expressed how much they disliked that their favorite tabby had to live in the cold, scary garage all by himself.

"Can't you just take an allergy pill, Mom, so that Friendly could live inside with us?" James asked (in his most *innocent* voice.)

"I'm willing to try that, James. But I don't think it's a good idea to let Friendly roam around free until we know, for sure, that the pills work."

"So, what are we going to do with him?" asked John.

"Wait!" James cut in. "I know you would have trouble sleeping here if Friendly lived in the house. But what if you were just here during the day to take care of us? Then we could get another house for you to sleep in at night. That way, you would be okay!"

Bill and I couldn't help but chuckle at the well-intentioned suggestion.

"I'm not sure that would work, sweetie. Besides, I want to live here with you boys and Dad! But I'll tell you what: we can try moving Friendly into the laundry room for now. How does that sound?"

The boys nodded enthusiastically, and everyone agreed that this new arrangement would be the best solution for the whole family. The matter was settled, and now it was time to break the news to Friendly.

John and James helped me move Friendly's toys into the laundry room, along with his litter box and food and water bowls. The doghouse had to remain in the garage, but I purchased a comfy cat bed so that he wouldn't have to sleep on the cold tile. To make it extra cozy, I lined the bed with the Marimekko quilt that had been in the doghouse.

Friendly watched with great interest as we moved his possessions inside the house. He seemed to understand that he was getting his wish and purred to express how happy he was.

The transition was seamless. Friendly was thrilled. The boys were thrilled. I was relieved. We had finally found a viable solution for our one remaining tabby. As for my husband, he was just happy to have his garage back...but had failed to anticipate what he would lose *next*.

The laundry room was the only way to get from the garage to the rest of the house unless we went outside. It was also the only way for Bill to get to his office, which was adjacent to the washing machine.

Now that Friendly was living in *that* part of the house, Bill had trouble accessing his office without the kitten running in to play on his desk. It was also difficult for anyone to go in there without Friendly attempting to escape into the rest of the house.

Just days after moving indoors, our furry friend had set his sights on taking over our entire home...and was *well* on his way to doing so.

2 1

IF THE LAUNDRY ROOM IS BETTER,
THE REST OF THE HOUSE IS BEST

F riendly loved his new quarters, but he also knew that
beyond the laundry room door was an *even nicer setup.*
There were soft sofas, warm and comfy beds, and a family of
four that would snuggle him whenever he liked.

Every time one of us opened the door from the kitchen to
the laundry room, Friendly would leap down from his perch atop
the cabinets. Then, using the washer as a springboard, he sailed
through the doorway into the main part of the house.

From there, he would make a mad dash through the kitchen,
take a sharp right turn to run down the hall, then skid around
the corner to the staircase. He then bolted up the stairs, raced
down the hallway to John and James' rooms, and scrambled
under the lowest bed (or behind the heaviest piece of furniture)
that he could find. At which point, he would wait for someone to
discover, and return, him to his home in the laundry room. This
was Friendly's version of CATCH-ME-IF-YOU-CAN, and he savored
every moment of it.

His other favorite game was venturing into Bill's office to see
what he had left out on his desk. Friendly loved to play soccer
with any pen he could find and enjoyed batting around the many
paper clips scattered across the desk's surface. There was also a
big, overstuffed sofa in the corner that created the perfect spot

87

for lounging and taking naps. Of course, anytime Friendly went in there, he always made a mess of things...which Bill was *never* happy about.

"First, I lost my garage, and now I've lost my office. I can't take it anymore! We have to move this cat somewhere else," he said one night at dinner.

"Yeah Mommy, poor Friendly shouldn't have to live and sleep alone in there," James chimed in.

"He could sleep with us in our rooms! Then we could cuddle with him all night!" John added.

Once again, the pressure was on me to let Friendly have full run of the house. This was an important decision. Would we continue to keep him in the laundry room? Or was this little tabby about to become an official member of the family, with all the privileges that come with it?

Of course, I loved Friendly just as much as the boys did, and I felt terrible that we couldn't let him into the house all the time. Even Bill had grown fond of the tabby and didn't want to see him leave. (He just didn't like that Friendly was taking over *his* parts of the house.) But I was too allergic to give in to the rest of the family's wishes, and it didn't make sense to put myself at risk over this. Besides, cat hair gets *everywhere!* It would be nearly impossible to remove from the furniture and carpet, not to mention the air inside the house. It just wasn't worth it.

Friendly had only moved into the laundry room a week earlier, and I was barely surviving. The longer he remained in the house, the more trouble I had.

I could have dealt with the sneezing and itching, but I struggled to breathe once the cat dander entered my lungs. Every time it happened, I was reminded of the slumber parties I had attended as a teenager and the severe reactions to my friends' pets. It was now becoming obvious that it would have to be either me or the cat. We couldn't both continue living under the same roof.

Despite that logic, I desperately wanted things to work out so that Friendly could stay. So, I announced that I would make an appointment with my allergy doctor the next day — to explore the possibility of desensitization shots. *At least then I could say that I had exhausted all possibilities.*

MY APPOINTMENT with the allergist was disappointing from the start.

"I'm sorry, Liz, but I just don't think that desensitization shots will work on you. Your allergies are too severe," the doctor explained.

"Even if we could do it, the protocol takes many weeks. During that time, you can't have *any* exposure to cats or dogs. So, you would have to find some place for the cat to stay."

"I was afraid you were going to say that."

"You've been taking those allergy pills I prescribed, haven't you? How are those working?"

"Well, I take one in the morning when I first wake up. And I take another before I go to bed at night. They worked just fine when the cats lived outside, but now, they don't seem to be as effective," I replied.

"I know this isn't what you want to hear, but it's my professional opinion that keeping this cat is only going to make things worse for you. You're already uncomfortable as it is. My concern is that if this continues, you will end up in the hospital because of your asthmatic reactions. There is nothing I can prescribe that will get you to the point where you can live with a pet."

There it was. The news I had dreaded from the start. But the doctor was right. I couldn't go on like this.

"Yes, I agree with you, and I appreciate your counsel on the matter," I said as I got up to leave.

"I'm sure you will be able to find a good home for him," he encouraged.

"Yes, I'm sure we will."

Driving home from the appointment, I couldn't help but feel disappointed. I was sure that the doctor would have a magic bullet so that we could keep Friendly. However, life does not always work out the way we expect it to.

I wish I could have pointed to a different reason as to why the kitten couldn't stay. For instance, if we didn't have enough space or couldn't afford to feed him. Yet I was the only reason we couldn't keep Friendly. Sadly, there was nothing else that could be done about the allergies.

At this point, I was finally coming to terms with the fact that it was time to find a home for our last remaining tabby.

22

TIME TO FIND A NEW HOME

The morning after my doctor's appointment, I was getting ready to take the boys to school. In a hurry to get out to the garage, James threw open the door to the laundry room, allowing Friendly to run into the house.

Together, we checked the usual hiding places but Friendly was nowhere to be found. Worried that we would be late for work and school, I told the boys to leave the tabby to his own devices for the time being.

I'm sure Friendly was delighted to have the whole house to himself. Had he been able to speak, he would have told us of the exciting adventures he had while exploring every room.

By the time we returned home that evening, our little friend was found curled up on John's bed, in the midst of a blissful nap. Nothing was amiss nor were there scratches on any of the drapes or furniture. He had faithfully used his litter box and had been on his best behavior all day long. *He really was the ideal house cat.*

The only problem was that there was now cat hair *everywhere,* which meant that I had to breathe more rapidly to get enough air into my lungs. Within minutes, I could feel my throat start to close up and began gasping uncontrollably. I quickly walked out on the deck to get some dander-free air. John and James followed me out to see if I was okay.

"I'm sorry, boys. Friendly can't keep living here," I said between wheezes. "We are going to have to find a new home for him...*and soon.*"

I think it was then that they understood the severity of the situation. Even though I had told the family what the doctor said the day before, I'm sure they were still holding on to some sliver of hope. However, once they could see how much trouble I was in, they agreed that a new home for Friendly was the only possible solution.

The rest of that evening was bittersweet. We all reminisced about how Friendly, along with his brothers and sisters, had been born in a hole in the tree, at the edge of our backyard. We laughed over Junior's standoff with the raccoon and got choked up when we talked about Momcat disappearing. What an adventure these tabbies had taken us on!

I was convinced that our last special kitten would go on to live a wonderful life with a very special family. I had the feeling that everything would work out for Friendly. And, by the end of our conversation, the boys began to believe that too.

"We just have to make sure that we find a good home for him...and that his new family is nice," James said.

"I promise we will find the best possible home for him," I responded, trying not to cry.

Of course, none of us wanted to see Friendly go, but we knew it was necessary. Besides, the longer we kept him, the harder it would be to say goodbye. He had such a wonderful personality that you couldn't help but get attached.

Friendly was incredibly affectionate, wanting nothing more out of life than to be a house cat and enjoy endless cuddling and playtime. He was also quite the talker.

Whenever any of us addressed him, he would answer with several *meows.* Every meow conveyed a different meaning, which the boys and I quickly learned how to interpret.

If you placed food in his bowl, he communicated a clear *thank you* — just like his mother used to do.

If you had to pull him from one of his many hiding spots, he meowed in protest.

If you invited him to sit in your lap, he would let out a deafening purr, his whole body vibrating in delight.

Then there was his sweet little face, which would light up as soon as he saw you. In fact, I'm convinced that his mouth was constantly tipped up in his version of a kitty smile.

However, the fact remained: I could no longer continue to live in close quarters with our furry friend. So, the first call I made — in my quest to find Friendly a new home — was to the veterinarian. I figured that he might know of someone in need of a loving feline companion. While he couldn't identify a family right away, he said he would make some calls and get back to me.

In the meantime, John and James' classmates had all grown very curious about the day-to-day happenings of the cat family. They were always eager to hear stories and updates about Momcat, Junior, and the rest of the kittens. Some had even seen photos of the tabby bunch and were eager to take Friendly home to be their pet.

Between this and the vet, it was only a matter of time before we would find a new family to give him to.

23

SAYING GOODBYE

One day, James came home from school and told us a sad, but promising story.

A little girl in his class had confided in him that her cat recently died. Both the girl and her family were, understandably, deeply saddened by this loss and had started their search for a new pet.

Upon hearing this, James, with mixed feelings, immediately thought of Friendly. He told the little girl that his mom couldn't live with cats in the house because of her allergies. Because of this, we were looking to find a new home for the last of our kittens.

This news seemed to lift the girl's spirits, and she said she would go home to talk to her parents about it. Meanwhile, James came home to consult with us.

"So, what do you think, Mommy?" he asked.

"I think you may have found a home for Friendly," I replied.

James agreed.

With that, I gathered up some pictures for him to bring to school the next day. Then I wrote down my name and number so that the girl's family could reach out if they were still interested.

TO MY SURPRISE, the mother of the family called me the same day that James delivered the pictures to the little girl.

"We are very interested in adopting Friendly, and would like to come over and meet him," the woman said.

I felt my heart sink into my chest. The word "adoption" was difficult for any of us to say, let alone hear. Of course, part of me hoped that we would never find a family for Friendly. Meanwhile, the other, more practical part was saying, *you have to find a new home for him, or you will end up in the hospital.* (Why, of all the possible allergies to be born with, did I have to be allergic to cats?!)

But after a few minutes on the phone, I learned that the family lived in a nearby subdivision. Not only that, but they seemed like they would take good care of our beloved Friendly.

We agreed that they could come over for a quick visit that Saturday and see where things went from there.

SATURDAY MORNING ARRIVED all too quickly. Before we knew it, there was a knock on the door. There they were: Friendly's soon-to-be family.

I invited them into the living room, where Bill and the boys were waiting to say "hello." James' classmate, along with her older sister, sat down next to him, while the parents sat over by Bill and me. Meanwhile, John ran to fetch Friendly from the laundry room so that everyone could officially meet.

"So, this is the kitten we've heard so much about," the father said.

"Yep, here he is," said John, holding Friendly close.

"Did you hear about the time he fell into the window well?" James asked. "I had to rescue him!"

The older sister, of course, had yet to hear the story. So, James relayed the tale, in a somewhat comedic fashion, while the girls went over to pet Friendly and get better acquainted.

Afterward, I gave the parents the essential information, like how he still had his claws but never destroyed anything. I also mention that he had been born in a tree but had no problem adjusting to life indoors.

Friendly, for his part, seemed to understand what was going on. He did everything he could to make a good impression on this family, as they would likely be an important part of his future. And it worked!

Friendly's inherent charm had won over the entire family by the end of their visit. However, they wanted to go home and talk things over before making a final decision. So, we all said our goodbyes and parted ways for the time being.

After the family left, the boys and I all agreed that they would be a good fit for our beloved tabby. Friendly seemed to get along well with the girls and their parents, and we all knew that he would receive lots of love and affection from them.

THE NEXT DAY, we received the call: *The family would love to adopt Friendly!* They asked if they could pick him up that evening and the matter was settled. After I hung up, I went to find John and James to deliver the news. Naturally, they were in the laundry room, playing with their best friend.

"Hey boys, Friendly's new family called and told me they would stop by later tonight to pick him up. I know it's sooner than we anticipated, but they are eager to make him part of their family."

The news caused tears to well up in their eyes, but both boys nodded to show that they understood. *This was the way it had to be.*

John and James' little mouths began to tremble as they uttered their goodbyes and gave their friend several long hugs. It was heartbreaking to watch.

I think we expected that it would take longer to find Friendly's new home, so there were mixed feelings about his sudden adoption. But this was meant to be.

In many ways, I was relieved to be freed from the burden of my allergies. But I was also devastated over having to say goodbye to the last of the tabby family. It wasn't just about giving Friendly away; this marked the end of the whole *Momcat and Junior Saga*.

From the first moment Momcat showed up on our back deck, I knew she would add a spectrum of color to our suburban lives. All the events that had since taken place, over the course of the past year, had been so unexpected, yet also very special and endearing.

Knowing that this chapter in our lives was about to come to a close was difficult, but I was still grateful for the time we had with the cat family and for all the memories they had given us.

The rest of that day was spent with Friendly, smothering him with lots of hugs and kisses and also packing up a few of his toys.

When the family arrived to pick him up, they assured us that we were welcome to visit any time to play and cuddle with our dear friend. This comforted all of us and made it a little easier to say our final goodbyes.

EPILOGUE

The boys and I took the family up on their offer to visit the very next day. We all needed some cheering up, and both John and James were adamant that we check-in to see how our little friend was faring in his new life. (The family, of course, was very understanding, especially given that they had recently lost their cat of 14 years.) Little did we know that, not only had Friendly realized his lifelong dream of becoming a house cat, he had won the lottery of cat living!

The house that the family lived in was more like a mansion. It had over 7,000 square feet of space, including seven bedrooms and seven baths. Even the ceilings were 20 feet high! It was all *quite* luxurious.

According to Friendly's new mother, their family had once had a live-in nanny to help take care of the girls early on. However, now that both girls were enrolled in school full-time, there was no need for one. That said, the family had originally designated one wing of the house for the nanny to live in. The wing had its own bedroom, bathroom, and laundry room.

After she was no longer there, they had decided to let their cats have that space instead. Now that Friendly was part of the family, this meant that he was the sole tenant of that entire wing of the house!

When the mother showed us his new accommodations, the boys and I couldn't help but chuckle at Friendly's newfound fortune, especially given that he had been homeless only a few months before.

Here was a kitten that had been born in a tree and had spent the better part of his life with no home, except for the space under our back deck. In a matter of weeks, he had graduated from living under the deck to the garage, and then to the laundry room. And now? He had a spacious bedroom — complete with a queen-sized bed, a side table, and an enormous comfy chair — all to himself! (There was no cat bed, specifically, so we assumed that the queen bed was where he took his naps.)

The litter box had been set up in the adjoining bathroom, which, of course, also had its own sink and shower. Down a short hallway was the laundry room, where Friendly could venture in, and out, whenever he wanted. This was also where the family had set up a water fountain for him to drink from, as well as a big bowl of *Fancy Feast* that was filled to the brim.

Beyond the beautiful accommodations, Friendly was free to roam around the rest of the house as he pleased. According to his new mom, he frequently gravitated toward any room where a member of the family was — to seek out snuggles and attention.

Based on what we could see, Friendly seemed to be adjusting quite nicely to his new life here. In fact, he looked happier than ever. This reassured us that we had found the perfect home for our dearest furry friend, and we left feeling that all was right with the world.

LIFE RETURNED to normal after that. While we never went back for another visit, the last we heard was that Friendly had grown up to be a beautiful tabby. Best of all was that he had undoubtedly become a lap cat to a very loving family and would spend the rest of his days in this very large house.

This was a true rags-to-riches story. (The world works in

funny ways, doesn't it?) And as Friendly showed us, even a cat with a dream can one day get his wish...*and then some.*

THE END

ACKNOWLEDGMENTS

As the title of the book suggests, this is a true story. It describes approximately nine months in the life of my family. In the story, I am both the mom and the storyteller. There is also my husband of 53 years, Bill, and — at the time the events took place — our two school-aged sons, John and James.

The story itself is set in a quiet but charming suburb of Chicago back in 1989.

Momcat and her family had an enormous impact on ours. For years, I've wanted to write her story, but always found that life's many responsibilities had a tendency of interfering with this goal.

Thirty years after the events unfolded, I finally found the time (compliments of the pandemic) to write about this special cat family, whose memory can now live on inside these pages.

Of course, as a fledgling author, I enlisted some help from close friends during the production of this book:

One key person that first spearheaded this project was Phil Dorman, a computer extraordinaire and good friend, who gifted the necessary technology (a Chromebook) to this novice writer. After a crash course on how to use it, I was compelled to type out the whole book, chapter-by-chapter.

My special thanks go to Annika Utgaard, an author herself,

who advised and counseled me throughout the editing, publishing, and launching of this book. With her guidance, my story became what it is today: a successful, in-demand title. Without her help, it would still be a manuscript sitting on a desk and would not have graduated into its current form.

As a result of the assistance and encouragement of these talented individuals, I had no more excuses *not* to write about my favorite cat family.

This book has been a true labor of love, and I hope that you enjoyed reading it as much as I enjoyed living it.

ABOUT THE AUTHOR

Elizabeth Downey is a wife, a mother, a grandmother, and the author of, THE CAT WHO CAME TO DINNER: A TRUE RAGS TO RICHES STORY. Having worked in the nonprofit sector since 1967, Liz is passionate about giving back to the community and the world around her. These days, she prefers to do this through writing and publishing feel-good essays about her unexpected encounters with animals. She also volunteers her time to help provide meals for those in need through a local church ministry.

Despite severe allergies to animals, Liz is known for being an observer and lover of wildlife. She is an unwavering animal advocate, finding innovative ways to protect any creature she crosses paths with. Liz also enjoys traveling and experiencing new things. In fact, she was able to get "up close and personal" with a mother lion and her cubs during a recent Jeep safari in Kenya.

As a Chicago-based author who enjoys interacting with her readers, Liz encourages those interested to get in touch by email at elizabeth.the.author@gmail.com.

LEAVE A REVIEW

What did you think of THE CAT WHO CAME TO DINNER?

First of all, thank you for purchasing this book. I know you could have picked any number of books to read, but you picked this one, and for that I am very grateful.

I hope that my story added some value and quality to your everyday life. If so, it would be wonderful if you could share the book with your friends and family on social media or at your next dinner party.

If you enjoyed this book and found some benefit in reading it, I would love to hear about it and hope that you could take the time to leave a review on Amazon or your preferred online bookstore. Your honest feedback will help readers determine whether this is the right book for them. Your support also helps me greatly improve my writing for future projects and will allow me to make the next edition of this book even better.

If you're interested, you can go to the book's product page on Amazon (or elsewhere online) and click WRITE A CUSTOMER REVIEW in the Customer Reviews section.

I want you, the reader, to know that your review is important to both prospective readers and myself. Thank you again for your support and feedback!